A Manager's Pocket Mentor

Mentoring is the shortcut to Experience.   Experience leads to better judgment, a better working environment, more satisfied and loyal employees.   This improves your success, your confidence, your happiness, and lowers your management stress and workload. You are now really good at your job, though it no longer feels like a job.   Sounds good?

Fred Gandolfi MBA PMP ®

Reviews and Recommendations

Does the world really need another management book? You wouldn't think so, but this little volume from Fred Gandolfi is so grounded in reality, down-to-earth, and full of practical advice, that any manager or aspiring manager should read it a few times and then refer to it time and again. This book reads just like Fred acts — direct, straightforward, and wise — and it delivers the manager's mentor that the title promises. Fred writes with such openness and humility that you can't help but be engaged. It would be better to have Fred as an in-person mentor, but for those of us not fortunate enough to work with him, this is a must-read book.

A quick scan of the table of contents may leave you puzzled at such a quirky set of topics. But there's a common thread to Fred's thinking: put yourself in the other guy's shoes and think about what would help him or her. Take his section on stock market basics. Now, what does that have to do with being a great manager? Directly, not much. But, indirectly, understanding how the market works helps you recognize that your executives, your customers, and your employees may all have different motivations. Even if, as he says, you can't solve the conflict in motivations, you can at least understand it. Put yourself in the other guy's shoes.

Fred takes on some of the most controversial and difficult topics for a manager in a modern corporation: layoffs, offshoring, differentiation among employees, resolving poor performance, and the constant change of today's business world. These are hard topics and Fred delivers common-sense, grounded advice.

With this book Fred has distilled his experience-tempered wisdom into a concise form that can help every manager. I know that I certainly will refer to this book over the remainder of my career.

Lee Nackman, Ph.D.
former Vice President of Product Development and Customer Support, IBM Software Group
June, 2011

Fred Gandolfi provides an invaluable reference book for both experienced and for new managers. He covers the important topics a manager should be familiar with, and addresses them in a personal and humorous way. Gandolfi learned his lessons from years of experience. With this book, he gives managers a fast start. This should be mandatory reading within the first month of a new management job, and be part of the annual professional development curriculum.

Hershel Harris, Vice President, IBM Software, Retired.
February 2008

Fred Gandolfi's book "A Manager's Pocket Mentor" tells like it is. No fluff, just straight talk. This resource paints the managers role from start to end. A very good read, to understand how a manager could approach work, and maybe more importantly, how an employee can understand why managers do what they do.

Andrew A. Czapran
Senior Consultant
Czapran Systems Inc.
March 2008

Mr. Czapran is an independent software consultant that has been working in the computer industry for over 20 years. His client list ranges over major banking institutions, large retailers, publishers and international organizations.

Introduction

Managers are drowning in impossible workloads, stress, caught in a bad sandwich between the Executives who seem to want a nuclear power plant delivered yesterday, costing pennies and the employees who feel overworked, underpaid, and underappreciated. The manager's work environment is toxic. It can wear you out.

And yet you know that the manager is the greatest influence on an employee's job satisfaction and morale. Morale leads to productivity, productivity leads to results. You as a manager have the single most important job in your company. Whether they admit it or not, everyone needs you to get it right. How can you succeed without losing yourself in the struggle? What has been tried before, what has worked?

People have consistently and repeatedly worked in a way that showed they thrived in the environment I provided. Leadership and Management were a natural fit for my value system and personality - because I think that leaders are leaders only when someone is willing to follow them, because I focus on the value people provide rather than what they cost. Establishing high performing teams exhibiting high morale comes naturally to me. But what was common sense to me, was also not normal. My approach to the job has often seemed to be special somehow.

I wrote this book on management to share ideas and advice that I have been providing in mentoring and coaching relationships over my career. The parts of the job that must be done well in order for you to be the kind of manager people enjoy working with.

These are the topics that I covered repeatedly with my protégés, distilled to the minimum that you need to know about them. It wouldn't cross my mind to buy a 200 page tome on Listening Skills. I would net such a book by "shut up and pay attention". Similarly, here I offer direct, condensed information on each topic I think you should master.

We all want to be validated, feel important and recognized. We all have so much talent inside, experiences by and large untapped. You and I are capable of much more than we do day to day. So is everyone around us. Think of the phenomenal untapped talent and dormant energy we carry with us every day, dulled by the incessant hammer of routine as well as possible futility of showing passion, life in a working environment where we assume it is not welcomed. A work environment you can and must improve upon.

You're probably reading this because you're a manager, a leader, someone doing the job that I love. I share with you my recipe for success – feel free to take what you want from it, to improve upon it as you see fit.

Fred Gandolfi
Markham, 2006

Acknowledgements and Dedication

First and foremost I thank my parents, Eduardo and Ana, for the uncompromising ethical values I use as the acid test in any dubious decision or situation I face as a manager. I believe that your integrity, your character and your charisma are what separate you from the leaders around you. I can't imagine having been successful in my career without the upbringing that I received.

I thank my wife, Jing, for the tremendous happiness, support, and love you've enveloped our home and my life with. I love the energy I have, the creativity I can tap into because I love my life, every day. You're a big part of it.

I single out Marvin Harrison for your tremendous support, friendship, and camaraderie during the many years it was my privilege to work for you. You have done so much for me personally, it's beyond description. You're a *mensch*.

I thank Ed Lynch for one day showing care and interest in my life and career, offering to be my mentor. Out of that generous offer and wisdom that followed sprung a noticeable improvement in my job satisfaction, the quality of mentoring I could offer people, and a greater efficiency and effectiveness achieving impact on the business.

I thank all the people I have managed, mentored, and worked with over the years. Your company and interaction made my job fun and meaningful. The insights from our social experiment make up this book. Since good judgment comes from experience, and experience comes from bad judgment – I ask for your forgiveness. In particular, I'm really sorry to the people who put up with me during my first year as a manager!

Fred Gandolfi

I wrote this book to break ground in the evolution of management – employee relationships, in the hope that the society you will one day work in will be better as a result, than the one I experienced. Thus this book is much more than my professional legacy: Vivien, Christina, Livia, Rachel, and Victoria, this is my gift to you, with love. Have a great life. Contribute to society and others, and make this world a better place for your kids.

Dad

What is Expected of You as a Manager

In a nutshell: "good government and more". Here's a checklist to get you started:

You need to provide a safe and respectful working environment, free from discrimination and harassment. The law helps you by making clear what is not allowed in the workplace. Common sense goes much further still. If you're a male manager and you are wondering whether behaviors around a female employee are proper and professional, pretend that she is your daughter. If you are wondering whether age discrimination is on your mind, pretend your parents are the subjects. It's that simple.

You need to provide clear direction of what is expected of people's jobs, so that they will know how to succeed in your eyes. People mean well, and by and large want to please.

You need to provide clear direction of how you will be evaluating their performance in as measurable a manner as possible. Share with them what checks and balances will be put into place.

You need to provide a framework for communication and status reporting. What data is required, what data is optional, when and how would you like to see it communicated?

How often would you like to meet as a team, and individually?

You need to explain to them your buttons (for e.g. honesty, integrity, money, time with family, project dates, etc). Find out theirs. It helps us get along and achieve common goals.

You need to provide a framework for decision making within the team, so that after the decision is done people support it and don't second guess it. The time for open, passionate and constructive dissent is before a decision is made, not afterwards.

You need to be the conduit of information from the rest of the organization to the team, and from the team to the rest of the organization. You are the advocate, both ways.

You must champion and lead them. You are their taskmaster, and also their biggest fan.

You must provide them with your support unless they prove it would be misplaced.

You must help their career, skills and experience growth. You are their coach. The more they can do, the more your team will be capable of and more fun you'll have.

You must validate their existence. Provide feedback (positive and negative) and recognition (positive only) in an objective, respectful, timely and fair manner. Typically feedback is provided in a private conversation, recognition in a public setting. If you value the relationship, have a care to deliver negative feedback verbally when at all possible.

You must not display favoritism. You also don't need to treat everyone the same – what motivates and pleases some, doesn't work for others.

You must take their side when they are at the limit of what is achievable and possible. That may mean standing up to your management on their behalf.

You must take on the responsibility of commitments made by the team to customers and other outside entities.

You must be able to admit when you made mistakes – and fix them.

You must procure what your people need to do their job in the most efficient and effective manner (equipment, safety gear, etc).

You must business case successfully the purchase of anything the team needs.

You must interview and hire excellent people. I don't mean skills, I mean character. Smart people can learn new skills, but you don't have time to fix bad character.

You must fire or remove incompetent or disruptive people. Never carry deadwood.

You must arbiter and eliminate ongoing destructive conflict. You must promote the occurrence of healthy conflict. Know the difference between the two.

You must provide an environment where learning from mistakes is expected, and judicious risk taking rewarded.

You must teach and uphold the fundamentals of project management. If applicable, endorse pursuit of certification from the Project Management Institute (www.pmi.org)

You must keep the team's attention on the customer and stakeholders.

You must prioritize ever increasing workload, and welcome dialogue on prioritization.

You must allow people to say "No" to you, with reason – leave the door open to debate.

You must celebrate accomplishments.

You must be supportive when life outside the workplace distracts the employee in the short term (death in the family, serious illness). Your good judgment will be tested here in terms of respect for the employee's privacy, and how long you carry them while they get their life in order.

Setting and Meeting Expectations

The moment I accepted and shook hands on my first management appointment, my new manager said to me the most valuable piece of management advice I ever received: *"your job is about the setting and meeting of expectations"*.

The manager-employee relationship, like any other relationship, requires the setting and meeting of expectations. The employee expects that for his efforts and results he'll be compensated and maintain job security, perhaps even receive awards and promotions. Through the proper setting of expectations he may also understand why there won't be a raise forthcoming, or expect to be fired from the job. If the manager communicates policy and expectations consistently and regularly, and provides regular status on his perception of how these are being met (or not) by the employee, then the employee and the manager are in agreement. There are no surprises, and everyone is safe in the relationship.

All games are fair, when you know the rules.

Do you punish an employee for the inefficient and ineffective way some task was done the first time, or reward them for getting it right the first time at all? Since project management involves a tradeoff of quality, time, and cost, do you reward or punish depending on which was inevitably sacrificed?

If you're in an organization where deadlines matter most of all, it would be a surprise to an employee that they got into trouble for submitting overtime claims for time worked to make the deadline. But in a company driven by budget, it would be surprising if an employee demanded overtime pay to cover the effort required to meet a deadline. Both instances involve the tradeoff between overtime and deadlines, but depending on the expectations of the job environment we have a much different assessment of what is appropriate behavior.

Setting and meeting expectations does away with surprises. This is important, as surprises in the workplace tend to be negative.

If your team knows evaluations will have much to do with the regular feedback given throughout the year, the evaluation meetings will be fairly uneventful regardless of the evaluation provided. If we know we're experiencing a hiring freeze for the next financial quarter, odds are that most employees won't be whining to you about understaffing. If you tighten down on travel and discretionary expenses, and disclose revenues are declining you may not have a hard time defending a smaller salary increase budget.

The intelligent people you hire will be supportive if you disclose relevant information, and educate them as to the challenges and expectations at hand. Setting expectations gets intelligent people on board with your agenda, and invites them to partner up with you.

Management Communication and Predictability

In my opinion, the manager is a constant feedback loop. He must be predictable in reaction to stress and other stimuli, so employees don't suffer from anxiety guessing whether the manager will get upset at certain news. This is of paramount importance because management requires data to make intelligent decisions, but employees won't provide accurate and timely data if they feel management lacks the emotional intelligence to handle it.

The manager
- sets goals,
- communicates to reaffirm the goals,
- asks for status and progress against the goals,
- takes steps to remove obstacles to the goals, and
- makes modifications in reference to the goals,

He keeps the organization focused on the goals, by ensuring the attention of the organization keeps coming back to them.

Once people find out that I value meeting dates above budget, people don't miss dates. Once they find that I value truth above good news, they tell me the truth and so save me effort I would have had to spend to find out "what's really going on". Once they find that I don't hold mistakes against people but instead value what we have learned from them, I see a team willingly sharing ways to prevent problems from re-occurring into the future. My predictability makes my team perform better and so makes us all more successful. This in turn feeds peer reinforcement: once some people in the team know what I would do they tell those who wouldn't have thought of it, and thus save me the time to educate them. Predictability is a wonderful thing. Strive for it.

Managing Your Workload

Whichever industry you manage in, it's likely that the biggest hurdle facing you today is how to manage your workload. Let me help you get control over your workload by netting out your Real Job.

What is it that you do? On what do you spend your time?	Provide as complete an inventory as possible of how you spend your time. Realize that you may be spending a non trivial amount of time on stuff that may not benefit your job. E.g.: walking to and from the coffee stand, chats on sports, politics, gossip to name a few (unless this time can be classified as networking)
What do you produce? Why?	Provide a list of the outputs you produce. This is what justifies your existence. The outputs need to be valuable – else your job is superfluous. You should be tenacious in your quest for valuable work for you and your team. Remember that tomorrow, today's accomplishments will be yesterday's news.
Who do you do this for?	Who is the most important among your stakeholders (boss, loudest customer, etc)? Typically it's the one who writes your evaluation. Ensure the person or entity you do your work for, is a motivating influence. If they're not, set yourself as the highest standard while waiting for a better stakeholder to come along.
How often do I need to do this?	If you do a task frequently any effort you spend on automation and process re-engineering will lead to time savings for you. If it's done once in a blue moon just document how it is done so the next time you need to do it you don't forget some important step. Frequent tasks require efficiency, infrequent tasks require effectiveness.
How well do I need to do this?	This is not the same as how well you can do it, or you'd like to do it, but rather how well it must be done. Learn the principle of Diminishing Returns. The difference between a $5,000 stereo speaker and a $10,000 stereo speaker is in the case of

	many purchasers mostly appreciated by their dogs. Unless you're a brain surgeon, strive for perfection on your own time. A company promising top quality at rock bottom prices is either selling a scam or going out of business. See yourself in the same light.
What happens if I don't do it?	Life is about choices and consequences; get candid on the consequences. Differentiate between your imagined fears and what is real and reasonable punishment in your organization. Remember always that you are a leader, and a professional. Your job is to break ground towards a better future. If you are constantly looking at your rear view mirror, chances are you are driving in reverse.
How much time do I spend on this?	Are you spending too little, or too much given what the task is worth? Your finite time is a very precious resource. Think of your time not as something to be spent, but rather something to be invested.

I promise you that if you spend a few hours on the activity above and guide your future actions accordingly, you will have a much lower workload problem in the future. This will differentiate you from many other managers. At a minimum, you will look less stressed and be more fun to be with. Professionally speaking, you will also be more alert, capable and willing to proactively identify, jump on, or create opportunities to increase the value of your team.

I work to the belief that every year we must achieve something that is much better than what was accomplished the year before. This is my contribution to progress. Where do I find time for this, never mind keep up with the job at hand? I constantly shave off the job the stuff that should not be done. This habit enables me to produce fantastic results.

Value vs. Expense

Marvels of technology and unprecedented levels of governmental cooperation on a global scale are constantly redefining what is possible today. As the playing field expands, you are also faced with the challenge of explaining to powerful people why you and your team ought to exist, costing what you do. You also need to explain it to your department so they see the value in what they do; then transform pride and purpose into morale, productivity, and results.

First of all, you must ask of yourself: "do I want to be in the commodity business or in the value business?"

If I sell oranges, how much can I charge for my orange? How sensitive are markets to my orange prices before I am replaced by another orange supplier? If I am the sole source of all oranges in the world, how price sensitive are my customers before they switch to another fruit type? There is a limit to what I can reasonably charge for an orange. An orange is a commodity: high volume, fairly indistinguishable, easily replaceable stuff.

Now let's assume that, God forbid, I am up for a heart operation. I may die on the operating table! Are heart surgeons a commodity? Are all doctors equally good, just because they all graduated? What if my surgeon was bottom of his class?

I have managed hundreds of testers across several countries. Is a tester a cost of doing business or part of the value chain? Many managers, accountants and executives will tell you they are a cost of doing business. But you are also a consumer. Would you buy again from a manufacturer who delivered you a faulty car or delivered a faulty car to a friend? What is your opinion on flying across the world on a plane whose systems testing was carried out by the cheapest qualified and certified labor available? Would you accept a slight surcharge on your airline ticket if they promised to check the wheel release mechanism twice? What if an airline company offered cheaper fares on planes checked every third flight, and most expensive fares on planes double checked every flight? Do you think Testing is a cost or a value proposition, now?

Fixing flaws after the customer finds them is seen by the customer as a cost, and by service teams as value. That is why companies charge for service, to fix the flaws they shouldn't have produced in the first place. **Customers however see value in the flaws getting caught or prevented before they use your product, while your finance department, management and executives see the money used for said prevention, as a cost.** The timing difference leads to a significant shift in perspectives, don't you agree? So, where do you sit? Is test a cost or an expense? Your employees, customers, pricing model and your business culture ride on your answer.

Offshore Jobs: A North American Perspective

In my opinion jobs shouldn't be sent offshore to save blindly on labor costs. After all you get what you pay for, and your customer may take a dim view if the product or process you have off shored no longer seems worthy of his money. Labor arbitrage is also a short term proposition as we witness the cost of living rising in the recipient countries. Then there are also setup costs, transfer costs, education costs, management costs, quality acceptance costs, communication costs… and lots of risks.

At the same time you must also recognize that about one third of the world's population resides in two countries that are presently among the top beneficiaries of the offshore trend. This one third of the world's population needs jobs, will increase in wealth, and for your sake better be a customer for your product. You can't hide your head in the sand and hope they all go to the moon. They are here, they are educated, and they are hungry for a higher standard of living. They are the heirs of a culture that was in decline long before your ancestors discovered the benefits of marrying beyond the confines of their village. They will not be denied.

When you see them as partners in global growth rather than leeches for your jobs, you see them as an extension of your labor force while you can dream up new and exciting products and services to grow your company. You have a vision of growth, and they may well be the ones who can staff it in the time required to make it a reality. The hired local talent may open doors to markets an order of magnitude larger than you're used to.

When you decide to make offshore sites part of your solution, keep in mind that you need to invest in them long term. These black holes sucking up North American jobs are suffering from growth pains, the specters of inflation and stagflation, and need your consultancy to grow successfully. You need time to create a joint culture where you both can speak about one topic and in the end recount the same story.

You must educate them on how to say "no" to you, or "this can't be done". Else you'll be set up in front of your sponsors, through miscommunication and inability to meet expectations. You must give the offshore teams interesting work and competitive wages, to attract their best people and not suffer from disruptive turnover. You must have a plan to occupy the labor force that is freed up in your home base, if you are to get their help to make the satellite teams succeed while growing your business though the success of both home and satellite teams.

Becoming "Offshore-proof"

While it's fine to speak of platitudes when it comes to jobs moving around the world, it's much more sobering and personal when the job that moves is yours, or of someone working for you. I have a global view of the economy, so I am not satisfied when I hear that in order to grow in one country, another country must go down. I don't believe in moving jobs. I believe in growing in both countries. When I have to work with people who can only think of the situation in terms of jobs moving between countries, then I work to prevent such moves.

My philosophy is simple: make the learning curve into my job and experience as high as possible. My job competence and complexity should be so high, that off-shoring my job would be tantamount to idiocy. It's not foolproof, but it improves the odds.

I strive to identify the parts of jobs that my people do, and classify them as "easy to transfer" and "hard to transfer". The easy-to-transfer portions I proactively work to eliminate through automation or process improvements. The hard-to-transfer portions I strive to make even harder to transfer by increasing their job impact, value and sophistication. I believe that in a service economy, people should be pushed to the limit of their intellectual capacity. When they work at this level they become indispensable and thus very hard to replace. Work that occupies their time that doesn't tax their intellect (I call this "grunt work") opens the door for boredom, disrespect for job and company, and increases the likelihood of off-shoring. This work I cut out as I would a gangrenous limb.

I am all for partnerships with other countries and cultures, but not by dismantling a successful local business. I believe in long term growth and prosperity, not the chasing of short term labor savings on a global scale irrespective of impact to the customer or loss of irreplaceable skilled labor in the "higher cost center". I believe that when you compete on price, you eventually end up producing garbage and stifling your long term growth as you will cut corners on internal investments your business needs to re-invent and modernize. I prefer to compete on value, because value commands a premium price. It takes better employees to understand and explain to customers the value proposition, but as a high performance leader you already know you should be forming high performance teams to handle such a job.

A while back it came up for discussion that cars from a certain North American manufacturer couldn't compete with the Japanese equivalents because the North American ones carried the burden of a $3,000 or thereabouts price tag due to employee pension cost, while the Japanese vehicle carried approximately only a $500 burden. The precise numbers themselves are irrelevant to me, so are the companies involved so they aren't being mentioned. Let's look at the implications, however:

One response to the above was a hue and cry that North American labor was collecting so much by way of benefits, that they were killing the company they were working for. Many took this view, and it helped fuel significant labor concessions in terms of wages, etc. Meantime I wondered: is it so bad for an employee to have a respectable pension after retirement? Of course not! So rather than figuring out how to emulate the Japanese with their puny pensions isn't the real question: how can we afford to have substantial, funded pensions?

So an alternative thought I formulated was: *who cares that the North American car has a higher pension driven cost component, if the employees are able to make a quality product that projects a higher value equal to or greater than this cost?*

You can buy a new car for $10,000, for $250,000, or any number in between; they all have four wheels and an engine, and can transport you at the legal speed limit. Clearly the minds and wallets of consumers would allow a car company to continue to pay for respectable pensions for their employees – if they produced the right value.

In-shoring Jobs: A Perspective from Outside North America

Jobs have been moving around the world, forever. Changes in consumer needs (spices, silks, purple dyes, pearls ...), technological advances (stone, iron, bronze, farming, shipbuilding ...), and economic inventions (commerce, money, banks, insurance...) among others have caused an ebb and flow of consumer goods and services, as well as the professionals who provided them, for millennia. You need to remind people who are insecure about your involvement, that there is nothing new going on and they should focus not on how you may be taking a larger share of the pie, but rather how both of you may make the pie bigger, together.

You need to empathize with an English North American culture that is for our purposes, in diapers. USA and Canada find it hard to think long term, because they are in their infancy both culturally and historically. Both countries have populations that seem relatively homogeneous, too. For e.g. Canada has two official languages, USA has a second unofficial language (Spanish).

If you're in India or China while you read this, you must be smiling. India has how many dozens of languages? India had an empire 1,900 years before the introduction of the horse into North America. China is over 3,000 years old. China gifted the world the main inventions of our civilization.

For the time being, your country enjoys the benefits of short term labor arbitrage, a lower cost of labor that will inevitable rise as the population learns to earn, spend, and demand higher wages in a natural inflationary cycle. In order to justify better wages and working conditions you will need to increase the quality of what you produce, and the stability of your trained and skilled workforce. You will also have to find a way to impress upon your North American parent company, that you are a worthy partner in the venture.

Remember your main argument when things go sour: it makes sense to keep investing in countries like India and China, because their consumer market is that appealing. And without consumers, companies don't grow. They have experience, technology, and infrastructure. You have the customer base. Aim for partnership!

Describing the Starting Point

You have been selected to receive a new project. In other words, you have funding to hire people, and also the responsibility to do something useful with them.

Your most important task initially is the hiring of good people as fast as possible.

You must educate the newly hired on the following:

- Company policy and culture (towards creating an impact team)
- Profession (skills, tools required to do the work)
- Product they will work on

Make sure everyone has an education roadmap, a buddy or mentor, and some initial responsibilities they can cut their teeth on. Give them work that helps them practice their skills on stuff that makes progress on the product being developed. Don't invent fictitious tasks. Nobody likes to waste time, everybody wants to contribute.

You need to familiarize yourself with the product plans for what you have inherited.

- What is the customer set?
- What are the key features?
- Who are the competitors?
- What are customers presently unhappy about? This is important; it helps you prioritize what to work on if you can't do it all.
- Who is your sponsor? Who is your boss? Hopefully you learn to please two masters quickly and painlessly – this necessary evil is referred to as "matrix management"
- When must you say "no"?

When to Say NO, and How it is Said

It's a recurring theme in cultural disconnects between North Americans and counterparts from Asia in particular, that we don't seem to find a common ground on what "no" means, and when it must be said.

Let's do a quick inventory of gross generalizations:

- "no" means "no" in North America
- "we are working on it" can mean "no, it can't be done, you're acting silly just by asking, but we're still on it to make you happy" in India
- "No" means "no" in China if it is said from the manager to the employee. It's not so clear when the employee will challenge the manager's "face" by saying "no" up the chain. Sometimes you get back a "smile", and that is not helpful in a phone conversation. Sometimes you get back half-hearted effort, figuring that time will make the request go away.
- *silence* means disagreement in Japan. Or you may see people getting up from their chair to sit further away from you, or loudly sucking in their breath. That's the Japanese version of an emphatic "NO". It's pretty funny when you realize than in North America, silence equates to agreement; people switch chairs only to find ones that are more comfortable, and making loud air sucking sounds during a meeting is merely a sign of poor manners.

Of course the problem is compounded when there are witnesses, and even more so when the witnesses are of varying degrees of influence. In a room with an Asian executive and five underlings, there is only one opinion that matters. North Americans forget this when they ask for brainstorming opinions, or worse a vote.

Lawrence of Arabia taught new British Advisors to ensure that in matters of disagreement, the Arab leaders had to maintain face. *"Keep discussions and disagreements with them, private"*. Know the culture of who you're dealing with, if you expect common ground and joint progress.

So when you, the Asian manager need to give status to your North American sponsor, keep this in mind:

- If you don't say "no", then it means "yes".
- If you don't say anything, it also means agreement.
- If you say "no", nobody lost face. They may get upset something can't be done, or disappointed. But your inability to do something was understood and your honesty, appreciated (I assume that you don't say no because you are risk averse, or disagree with the Executive direction – the only "no" that is allowed, is one based on inability to accomplish a task)

What happens when you don't say "no" to a North American, and yet that was the only valid answer to a YES/NO question? Simply put, you are deemed to have lied. You lowered yourself in their view as someone who can't be trusted and thus requires a future investment of painful micromanagement.

Catering to cultural differences is like giving presents to someone. If you know what you want the other person to have, you may purchase a gift accordingly. A much better present to give is the one the other person needs or wants, regardless of your personal preferences. In environments of marked cultural differences, learn what makes the other person happy. From there you can start the difficult job of how to team up on the problems at hand, whatever they may be.

Micromanagement

It is likely that the work that was given to you for managing is a product that was already performing properly, with an established customer base, maintained or developed by a finely tuned group of professionals. You are staffing this with a group of unknown skills and potential, with no demonstrated track record, and the business cannot be put on hold while you show you were worthy of this trust through any attribute other than your lower aggregate labor costs or physical proximity to a new customer base.

Naturally, the sponsoring group is concerned whether you will be able to deliver what you're supposed to deliver, without glitches in quality or missed commitments to customers. In the ideal world, the customer wouldn't have any idea whatsoever that the work moved countries. When we buy a product, our main consideration is that it works, right?

Until you demonstrate that your team can deliver without skipping a customer's beat, expect to be micromanaged. You will attend endless meetings to go over what was accomplished, what is to be accomplished, what gets in the way and what will you do about it. These meetings are expensive in time and resources for both countries!

Rest assured that your North American brethren hate these meetings. For all the micromanaging they can muster, it doesn't make you any more efficient or effective. There is a chance that your team is too busy preparing for the meetings, to be able to focus on the job at hand. When you learn to communicate status in a language you both can agree to, and your team delivers on interim deadlines with reasonable risk and predictability, these meetings will decrease in length and frequency. Nobody in North America relishes the thought of working far into the evening just to nag and pester you. They would rather sleep.

Make your goal the end of micromanagement. Earn the respect and partnership of your sponsors, who wish for nothing less than your success so they can get on with the other aspects of their jobs. When they fly out to visit you they would rather spend evenings touring your beautiful country, than being locked up in a room looking over your Quality projections and wondering which ones are likely to be come true.

Growth Pains

With success and new projects comes growth, and such growth can be dangerous and painful. The challenges facing your rapidly growing team are formidable.

You will be faced with the choice of hiring less than stellar people to meet hiring projection quotas, or falling short on the staffing curve. I suggest you wait for good people.

You will be faced with the necessity of promoting someone to management for every 10-15 people you hire. That is a scary prospect, they likely are not ready. Buy lots of copies of this book for them! ☺

You will outpace your infrastructure. The people who supply your people with desks, phones, computers, office space, cars, secretaries, etc. may not be able to handle all your needs. HR may have a tough time lining up interview candidates. You may not have enough time to see everyone you should, while at the same time looking into transferring projects into your country and figuring out how to keep delivering them.

You will need to leverage yourself through competent team leaders and project managers. They will require time and training. You may need someone from the sponsoring country to come live in your country for a year or two to teach your team.   Take every opportunity to find education for your people, so they learn to be self sufficient.

Transitioning your Focus from Critical Mass to Morale

Once the team has grown to the point where you have achieved critical mass – you now have enough people to be able to handle internal training, product delivery, and grow experience and skills in spite of turnover – your next challenge will be morale.   Critical mass gets the job done, but morale aims to achieve productivity.   This productivity will allow your people to deliver more and more with their time and resources, so you can keep growing the business as well as them.

Morale is also the key measure preventing potential turnover in your personnel.   It can also be the attractor of top people from outside your organization into your team.

The Power of Straight Talk

You must say what you think. You will act, measure, decide, and evaluate according to how you think, so I suggest your speech match your thoughts and actions. You ought to learn to control your vocabulary to attain maximum clarity and impact while removing from the message: cynicism, sarcasm, negativity, and anything that could be construed as unprofessional or detrimental to the nurturing of healthy, long term relationships.

To improve the odds that your point will be considered as you want, you must ensure you're not making the recipient defensive – especially if they outrank you. Stay as objective as possible and focus the conversation on the topic – not the person!

Straight Talk is required in your job because there is too much filling in the blanks on gaps in the communication. People will often hear something other than what you think you said, and *they will not take steps to validate their perception. You will not take steps to validate your assumption of what they heard.* This is a recipe for disappointment.

So work on your Straight Talk! When you want something, say so.   When you value something, say so.   When you expect something, say so.   When you are disappointed, say so.   When you are vehemently against something, say so (professionally).   No guessing, no innuendo, no subtlety.   Whenever you can't afford a misunderstanding, ensure you say what you mean, mean what you say, and you get feedback the message has landed as intended.

I admit that my Straight Talk is blunt on occasion.   I have been known to tell employees who tell me they should be evaluated highly for attending so many meetings, that the chairs in the meeting rooms attended even more.   This is followed by the explanation that I don't care what meetings were attended, but rather what was contributed by the employee to the meetings that were attended. How did their attendance impact the business?

Sometimes it is talk driven to change mindsets, paradigms.   At the end of a meeting with my leadership team, I recently asked: "do you think we will have the same number of people we have today, to do what we do in 5 years time?"   This opened up their minds, as intended.   Then I added: "I'd be surprised if we were not down 20% of the staffing we use today to achieve what we do."   (Uncomfortable silence follows)   "I suggest we figure out how to make our people 20% more productive before someone cuts us, and use the extra productivity to achieve something to impress our Executives so we're not cut to begin with".   For the next few days, some of my managers started their chats with me with "I've been thinking about what you said… I have this idea…"

I also use straight talk during monthly 1/1's, to call out exactly how we both feel about stuff.   This keeps the relationship very clean, very open, and minimizes surprises and misunderstandings.

I also use straight talk to lavish praise on my team and my top performers. I ensure those deserving special praise and recognition get that and then some. I go out of my way to tell them that they are the best and I am fortunate to have them in my leadership team. And of course I mean it!

As I see it, Straight Talk is about truth, honesty, reality, an invitation to engage in a higher order conversation. The point you want to make has to land on target, with a thud. It creates clarity, lets everyone know where things stand, and stimulates action.

A Template for Making Requests

A common failing in new managers communicating with their teams, is their inability at formulating effective and efficient, powerful requests. Here is an example of a template that works:

Bob, I require you to handle the preparation of this Special Bid (TOPIC, AND ASSIGNS OWNERSHIP).

The Bid must include all items we want to offer to the customer, the prices and discount levels approved by Finance, and an appendix from the Sales team that reflects what we know about the pricing for a similar offering by our top three competitors, A, B, C. (SPECIFIC INSTRUCTIONS AS TO CONTENT OF THE TASK AT HAND)

I require the Bid for my review by Wednesday 4pm, so I can turn it around to you overnight if something doesn't look quite right (BOB's DEADLINE).

If all goes well, I will send it to The Big Guy for final approval on Friday, so we can pitch it to the customer on Wednesday of next week (THIS INFORMATION IS OPTIONAL, BUT MAY BE USEFUL TO GET BOB'S BUY IN ON THE URGENCY AND REASON FOR HIS WORK, AND WHY YOU PICKED THE DEADLINE YOU DID)

I appreciate your help with this. Let me know if anything is not clear, and if anything gets in the way so I may remove it for you. (INVITES BOB TO SEEK CLARIFICATION WHILE THERE IS STILL TIME TO PREVENT HIM FROM GOING ASTRAY – OPENS THE DOOR TO HELP BOB ASK YOU TO REPRIORITIZE PREVIOUS COMMITMENTS) Thanks, Me.

Straight Talk from your Direct Reports to You

Straight Talk isn't just about how you communicate with your employees; it's also about how your employees communicate with you. You can start training them to give you the goods, right from the start.

A common error by rookie managers involves their running off to do what they think they should do with their new team, without first asking the team for their opinion. A very powerful application of straight talk involves asking all department members, individually and in private, for their honest perception of how things are going, what is going well, what is off the rails, and why. A great opportunity also to ask them to tell you what would make their environment even better than it is.

You will be pleased to know that through such meetings you will get rich guidance, data and reasons that will clearly point to the next step for the team, and what your next communication to management ought to be. Your employees are the experts; ask them what's going on before you go looking for ways to leave your mark.

Of course some employees are reserved in how much data, personal preferences, and opinions they will disclose to their new manager. That is ok; it takes time to build trust. Do tell them, however, that your decisions are only as good as the data and preferences you have at hand. You have no proven psychic abilities. If you end up making decisions that disappoint them, they'll have to live with the consequences. If you're genuine about it, and I can't see why you shouldn't be, then most of your employees will share with you more than enough for you to work with. When they see that good decisions came from this data, they'll be encouraged to trust you even more.

The Power of a Decision Making Model

In my opinion, the single most destructive factor leading to the unraveling of a team under your care is the lack of buy-in or acceptance to the decision making process used by the team. Add to this the subsequent disgruntlement and undermining of the decision by those who felt trampled by it.

It is not optional: you require 100% commitment from all members of your team to any decision made. You must hammer that into the team. Argue all you need to before the decision is made, but make a united common front after the fact.

What is up for grabs is how the decision will be made. Is consensus required? If not, do we need a majority? What constitutes a majority? 50% + 1 more person? Or X%?

If a majority is required and we agree how much, when is the earliest we can take a vote? Does everyone need to be heard? Do we limit discussion on the topic to 30 minutes? Does everyone need to be present at every decision? Do we allow voting by proxy?

Does your opinion as manager entitle you to more than just one vote? Do you get veto power? Does anyone get veto power?

How do we decide as a team when the decision must be made immediately (many requests from above the management chain require immediate answers)?

You must decide how to decide, before involving your team in decision making.

Layoffs

Since the 1990s, layoffs have become part of North American culture. Given the influence of American companies on the global economy, they are also affecting the entire world in some form – including positively through the creation of jobs as the layoffs savings are translated into investment elsewhere.

To me, layoffs are by and large an admission of management and leadership failure and of their giving up. Whatever the text of the layoff announcement, this is how my brain translates it:

"We at Company X know full well that we underutilize the tremendous talent present in our labor force today, talent we have spent immeasurable resources finding and training. But we have reached a point where we admit we are unable to figure out what else we can do with this talent. We know what it costs to keep this talent, but we can't figure out what we lose if it goes elsewhere. So we will pay them to leave, and likely they will go to our competitors. But the company will become stronger, fitter… blah, blah, blah."

I have a solid formal training in Corporate Finance and Organizational Behavior. I'm talking A+ solid. If you too have had the privilege of an MBA education from a top University, and have any amount of meaningful working experience to go with it, you too can spot the real cost of a layoff. As this is what will lead to your biggest managerial and leadership headaches over the next few months, let's look at the real cost. Let's look at your upcoming workload:

(a) Lower morale of the survivors – they miss some friends, they feel some survivor guilt, and don't want to pick up the work from those who were let go (they don't like the extra workload; makes them accomplices in the ousting of their friends)

(b) Lower productivity of the survivors, following from lower morale as well as the distribution of newly unmanned work

(c) Erosion of trust in management by employees. How did management choose who was to be laid off? Did management have a say? How long did management know about it? What else does management know now, that could be harmful?

(d) Erosion of trust in Executive by management (this is extremely dangerous – who leads the troops when the managers lose confidence?)

(e) Inability to align over the short term the productivity of the organization on the goals the Executive wants pursued (and how long to rebuild the communication channels, and trust?)

(f) Insecure or shocked employees (and I've seen absolutely brilliant employees who ought to never have feared the loss of their jobs, included in this group) irrationally stop doing productive work because they feel "they are next".

(g) People spending time brushing up their external contacts, polishing their resumes

(h) Decrease in voluntary overtime, ownership, commitment, and risk taking – as "there is no point to it, we're next", or "if the work mattered, the people who did the work wouldn't have lost their jobs"

The stock market sometimes rewards a company that has layoffs with up to a few days of a temporarily inflated stock price change. This is justified largely on the premise that "management is stepping up to the hard decisions". Very odd - don't the hard decisions revolve around how to get this "surplus" workforce productive, to grow the business?

Before a layoff, employees are loyal and focused on taking risk, achieving success, growth, and teamwork. Long term goals are valued and supported. After a layoff, employees no longer feel a tie to the company or team, and are out to improve themselves as individuals to be shielded from layoffs or possessing a better resume for when they eventually lose their jobs. Sometimes they lower their output in fear that work will run out, and they will lose their jobs. Short term goals become the order of the day. Risk is frowned upon, change not supported as it may increase short term risk. Extra tasks to make the company more competitive are paid lip service or outright ignored, as no employee wants to feel "used and discarded" once they're done. Managers are no longer worthy of trust, no longer merit the extra effort requested. This is exactly the opposite of what management intended while trying to make the company more competitive!

I'm not going to tell you layoffs are not necessary. I think they are, if large projects have gone away and won't be replaced. If a company is faced with insolvency, so some jobs will be saved through terminating others, buying the company time to rebuild. But it ought to be a method of last resort. It is a final admission of management and leadership failure. A visible collapse of yesterday's management strategy, or a reflection of marketing or production incompetence, or the result of unions or regulation squeezing the goose with the golden eggs so much that it just chokes. It should not be something that happens often, and management ought to resist any and all impulses to follow this path unless every other path has been proven unacceptable.

Early in my career, I was under the impression that layoffs were a phenomenon associated with companies in their death throes. They were out of money, they couldn't afford their buildings, and they were being driven to extinction by a competitor. So like a wolf in a trap, chewed the leg that was caught so to wobble away with three good legs and fight another day.

However, over the past few years layoffs have increasingly been used as tools to beautify the balance sheet, no longer just the action of last resort to stave off bankruptcy. And this, I have serious objections to. In my opinion companies that lay off to improve the balance sheet while profitable, are running a horrendous risk of a loss of productivity that will hurt them in the long term. This loss is due to declining loyalty, disenfranchising of the remaining employees. It's true that many things won't get done if they can't be measured; but it's not true that things that can't be measured don't exist, or can't hurt your bottom line. I believe that the negative side effects of layoffs on the surviving population are much more damning to a company's long term health, than the short term boost the layoffs meant to attain.

Assuming the Executives know all this, why then do they do what they do? It seems to me that as their compensation is so strongly linked to stock performance, they understand loud and clear that their primary job is to raise the price of the company's stock. They really have no choice. They don't get to run the company for themselves; they run it for the stock market analysts, the mob of financial advisors, Joe Trader who needs to hear good news if he's to keep his kid's University tuition money on the stock for another quarter. At every level in a company, it's tempting to look up and say "why don't they do the right thing!" But to be fair, the same can be said by those looking up at us. We don't know what constraints the Executives are under – we can only guess based on their compensation, and also on the repeated pattern of their behavior.

Whatever your personal views or arguments on the points I offered above, the crux of your problem is still this: *As a manager you will at times be called upon to justify stock price based layoffs to employees who aren't remunerated by stock, trying to keep them motivated to do their jobs for the sake of the customer who justifies our existence.* As impossible tasks go, this one is pretty much the worst. But it can be done. It has to be done. It's your job to get it done, and you better do it well.

I remember once defending a 5% pay cut to a team. The team was obviously unhappy, and so was I - how to maintain morale through this? So I laid it on the line: The Company needs to cut down expenses. We can't shed 5% of a building. So we have to lose 5% of our variable costs, i.e.: salaries and benefits. Does anyone here have a list of people we should lay off, so we can achieve 5% savings? I don't have the moral right to go picking such people myself. Do you have any names?

Ok, so since you don't, how about we all get a 5% cut in pay, almost half of which is taxes anyway, and we all keep our jobs? And when the company turns around, I'll go looking for raises? I was thrilled to see that my team had the highest morale when the entire area got hit with the 5% cut. They understood their value, their contribution to the company's long term health, and each other.

Roughly around the same time the Right Honorable Bob Rae, then Premier of the Province of Ontario, Canada, came up with his Social Contract. It made public sector employees take extra unpaid vacation days, to save the government payroll money. The unions were furious. But Premier Bob Rae, I argued with acquaintances in the government sector, had given his employees a gift! His employees had a pay cut just like mine, but they got vacation days off for it. They actually didn't get a pay cut in terms of pay for hours worked! Meanwhile I had to work every hour for less pay.

It's not about management vs. employees, or management vs. unions. It is about the creative use of power, and of the talent at hand to solve common problems for win/win long term. For respectful treatment of everyone, while maximizing the value for all stake holders.

When you do resort to a layoff, keep in mind the culture in your company is about to undergo firing at the forge. You're on damage control now. Good luck with it.

Counterpoint: An Executive's Perspective

It's important to learn from the different perspectives available to us. I got this view from a review on this section by an Executive I respect and admire:

"Your opinions on Layoffs don't reflect mine. You're right that it is traumatic and difficult, and the last thing a business wants to consider. But as part of "the only constant is change" I believe it's sometimes the right choice, and the sooner the better. Employee imbalances can need quick hiring, retraining, or firing to correct, and can happen from external market, competitive changes, or technical advances that are a part of doing business. I only provide a more moderate view – you're welcome to yours".

This is an insightful perspective on layoffs. It is the job of the executive to ensure that the company proactively and nimbly hops around from opportunity to opportunity, minimizing costs and maximizing returns. I guess that it comes down to a window in time. Is the labor force re-trainable in the short timeframe required? How quickly can it be retooled? How quickly can it adapt to the changing needs? Is it realistic to expect that the expert buggy whip makers become competent car engine designers? Often times, sadly, no.

In light of this, I suggest for the manager to remind employees (and herself), that it is their duty to stay marketable in the chosen industry and product sector. They must be able to demonstrate value add to their chosen profession and customer set. They must be able to make high impact customer presentations, and be acknowledged as the experts and leaders in whatever chosen pursuits. The executive quoted above saw layoffs as a last thing for a business to consider – but the time spent considering it, kept short by necessity. Is it like ripping off a band-aid, the faster the removal, the less the pain?

Many of us will be faced with the difficulty of deciding "when to give up" on projects, studies, several times in our careers. When do you give up on your current job, and seek a new job? When do you stop coaching a low performing employee and start the process to fire him? When can you say for certain that you have tried enough at these things and others, confident that an extra month or twelve would not have made a difference? It's hard. Executives get to the decision, faster. Their experience and contacts in the field maximize the accuracy of their decisions under significant uncertainty. They want to make right choices too.

I don't like exposing myself to the vagaries of someone else's decisions. It bothers me to have someone decide my future. This puts an onus on me to take charge of my life, decide what makes me happy and marketable, free to pursue what I want to pursue within reasonable limits. I believe that people who take charge of their lives, and keep themselves focused and marketable, have little to worry about in the long term. Society will hiccup along the way thanks to politics, markets, industry life cycles, etc. It's up to you and me to adapt and proactively get ready for the next change, seizing it as an opportunity. Layoffs, pervasive as they have become, can be seen as a mandated starting point for your new job and career. So re-tool in anticipation. This re-tooling may even make you so marketable that your company won't stand the idea of laying you off. Remember that companies do what they do to win and evolve. If you're part of your company's plan for the future, you'll do fine.

The Value of a Current and Impactful Resume

I ask every person reporting to me to have a current resume. I assure them that I have one, too. Because I expect each and every one of my employees to know they are marketable, and worthy of their employ and remuneration. You can do a lot with employees who are confident and know what they are worth. In our service economy, our worth is dictated by our marketability. Skills must be current, experience relevant, and customer contact frequent and impactful.

First, you need to collect stuff worthy of a resume. I have: two relevant degrees, a professional certification, patent submissions, a publication, this book, a list of awards. I have experience managing and leading very large teams across a number of countries. I have a track record for successful customer advocacy and relationships. I make compelling sales, and motivational pitches. I have invented stuff that was years ahead of its time, that is changing my industry. I speak several languages.

To ensure it was compelling, I asked a Vice President look over and critique my resume so that it does justice to my ever growing track record of running vital businesses with efficiency, effectiveness, high morale and customer impact on a global scale. I list only executives as references across several groups and companies.

See your resume as living proof that your company is lucky to have you. Read it often, feed your ego. You are special, priceless. There will never be another like you. Get your confidence into high gear, and go improve the world! Feed the resume your new accomplishments every 3-6 months, and revel in your glory as a leader and agent of progress. With this and a positive attitude, the high morale you are in charge of, you will love what you do and so will the people around you. And they call that work. ☺

Evaluation System

You can't evaluate the people reporting to you.   But you must evaluate their results.

Writing an Evaluation

I have evolved this format over the years – I find that it works very well for me:

Overall, Joey did / did not do as we agreed earlier in the year. (OVERALL ASSESSMENT)

Joey was responsible for these things, in order of importance: (list them).   Some were high risk (list), some low risk and expected to be done as part of the job (list them). (RECOGNITION OF JOB DUTIES, AND THEIR RELATIVE PRIORITY / DIFFICULTY)

For the above, item X was done / not done in terms of complete / on time / on budget. Repeat for items. (DETAILED ASSESSMENT)

The following things were taken on in addition, and we should recognize Joey went above and beyond (IT'S FAIR AND PROPER WE DO SO, BUILDS OUR CREDIBILITY TOO)

Beware of: "Joey would have done better if he'd... "   Sometimes Joey will take offense to see his perceived flaws in writing for future managers to read out of context.   So maybe you should tell Joey how to improve in another meeting, or during the evaluation meeting but not in writing, and only after he gives you permission he would like to hear it now.   It may not be welcomed now, and it's not necessary to today's evaluation anyway.

Generally, when writing an evaluation:

1. Less is more.   Say what you have to, back it up, and stop.
2. Don't use adjectives. Things were not done *very well*.   They either got done, or they didn't.   On time, early, or late.   On or off budget.   The result will be dry and boring, but the evaluation is not the time to practice prose.
3. Don't think of it as the time to build a relationship.   Either you had one before the evaluation, or you will build one afterwards.
4. Keep in mind the recipient of the evaluation is looking for validation that you understand the job being evaluated, the priorities faced during the year, difficulties of the tasks assigned.   You may disagree on the value of the results, but do you at least agree on the job at hand?
5. The recipient of the evaluation is looking for validation that management was fair and objective.

6. The recipient of the evaluation is looking to see whether the evaluation matches the ongoing feedback during the year (evaluation time is not the time to start giving feedback).
7. Remember the evaluation text may be used by lawyers in a Court of Law or by the Human Resources department during conflict resolution. You only get to write it once. Then it is out of your hands.

Never ask an employee to evaluate themselves!

- It is management's job to evaluate.
- The employee has a more limited view of their job than the manager, in the context of the wider company needs.
- It's likely that the employee lacks objectivity on their personal achievements.
- It is quite possible that the employee is more of an expert at their job than the evaluating manager – the debates following could be destructive
- The employee could be offended if the manager would argue the evaluation. After all, this was the employee's evaluation, not a test as to whether the employee could come up with an identical view to management's (I know of an instance when a valuable professional went job hunting and switched companies soon after such an experience – an avoidable waste).

Now that we know how to write evaluations, let's look at the Evaluation System itself. What is it trying to do?

A proper evaluation system, in my opinion, defines what is expected and allows for the recognition of how close we got to it. It also helps recognize extra as well as inadequate contribution. It ought to be backed up by clear goals, and measurable objectives.

It ought to complement the company compensation plan, by listing criteria for differentiation between employees. This helps you allocate the limited funds of your salary and bonus plan later on with a clear conscience.

The evaluation system helps reinforce the cultural values of your organization.

Evaluations generally should focus only on results. The evaluation is about what results (and impact) were attained through effort, not the effort itself. No University report card says "Johnny tried very hard to become a good doctor and so did lots of homework all semester". Instead it gives a grade.

We all have personal experiences involving unfair professors, unfair managers, who gave us evaluations we didn't deserve. Or just as bad professionally, managers who gave us evaluations we expected but for the wrong reasons. We all remember the lack of respect we had for those authority figures and the system they represented. So be careful, your integrity and competence as a professional and an evaluator are also being tested.

Performance Management, or Bottom Management

These are two of the many labels given to the sundry activities aimed at employees whose results are trending towards the bottom of the group, and may soon head into unacceptable levels whether or not legislation or contractual obligations let you do something about it.

A key question related to Performance Management: Are you evaluating the employee to help them turn around and produce improved results, or to ease them into separation from the business?

This is not a trivial question. There are quotas to be filled for the number of employees to be separated from the business every year in many companies – but I have yet to hear of a single company that measures how many troubled employees got turned around into successful and contributing members of the team. It says a lot about the lack of organizational forgiveness and the throw away culture we live in, that it is often expected of the manager to do what is required to demoralize the "bottom" employee into giving up and leaving, or accept a severance package without causing trouble or fuss.

Often times such a separation is best for the employee whether they realize it or not at the time. They are a poor fit to the values of the company culture, and they normally end up happier elsewhere and with a cheque in hand to boot. But it is a painful process, and few are the employees who won't see it as an inhumane crushing of their self worth.

As an aside, if you think you are impervious to the effects of firing someone, just imagine you encounter them and their family a few months later while shopping for groceries. Or their kid and your kid end up in the same class, so you meet at birthday parties. So don't get cavalier, you'd be amazed what a small world this is.

To carry out needed performance management, you are required to clearly define a minimum contract that the employee must meet to justify continued presence in the workplace. You need to have associated measurements so that a 3rd party may validate a pass or fail decision if required, and you must clearly and regularly provide feedback on whether or not the output meets expectations. It also requires the setting of a date by which a final pass/fail decision will be made. The time period ought to be long enough to document consistent progress or failure. Talk to your HR representative.

We manage human beings who at any time may have a less than perfect fit with the current needs and prevalent metrics of the organization. Evaluate the package that person provides with the flawed metrics at hand, your limited wisdom, and what the company at the time requires of them – but never lose sight of their humanity and their worth as people. Think how you would want to be judged yourself.

Management as an Agent of Change

When people face uncertainty, they usually become afraid.

But if our technological advances have taught us anything these past hundred years or so, is that the only constant in our lives, is change. The world is unfolding as it should, whether we choose to participate or watch it happen.

Change is pervasive, and its ongoing impact, permanent. I can't imagine my life without the Internet, and yet I was alive during a time when it didn't exist. There was a time I paid my bills by lining up at a Bank during lunch. Recently I found out my bank branch moved a few years ago. I don't know where it moved to, nor do I care. I used to ask people for addresses and directions, but thanks to technology an address is good enough now. For the directions, I use www.mapquest.ca . I wonder how the GPS systems for cars are affecting that business too, as I write this. I know people who don't wear watches anymore, because they read the time off their cell phones. I don't know anyone who owns a typewriter. I expected to explain to my kids one day what a vinyl record was, but I underestimated the topic – I was asked what a CD was, instead. Yikes! Have you tried buying an alarm clock radio without a built in MP3 docking station? I could write so many pages just touching on topics that have changed in my life over the past five years. Change is the only constant in our lives.

A manager must be an agent of change; the influencer of which change to embrace and support, align the team to, and mine new and exciting opportunities from. Change is our friend in that it provides solutions and answers to problems, new ways of doing things that enrich our lives. It forces us to grow up, learn and stay vital and valuable. It allows us to increasingly add value to ourselves, employees, other stake holders and customers. It keeps us vibrant and competitive, strong, flexible and agile.

Management can guide the team safely through change, by showing the positive side of change and negative consequences of the status quo. With change comes some risk. Management identifies risk, puts risk mitigation plans in place for those risks with unacceptable impact or high probability of occurrence.

There are some things that shouldn't change. You should never lose focus on your customers and your competitors. Never lose sight of legislation and contractual obligations.

Progress requires us to test the best known method for doing something in the most efficient and effective manner possible. Of course the main obstacles to achieving such a change, of identifying holes in the process currently in place are the people who were rewarded for establishing the current system in the first place - maybe even your boss. So be careful how you go about justifying the need for change. Generally people will sign on if you show what they will gain from the change, much more readily than if you attack the obvious flaws of the current system that they created.

Other benefits of change include

- Helps pass the time
- Avoids stagnation
- Can lead to team building
- Maintains fresh and current communication
- Trains the team into constant lookout for continuous improvement
- It's fun and rewarding to constantly find better ways to do thing
- Feeling of accomplishment for whoever came up with the idea, and the solution
- Everyone can contribute to a better future
- People become less afraid of what is in the end, inevitable
- You sharpen your leadership skills
- You deliver more value, pleasing your sponsors
- You transition from Management into Leadership, which is a lot more rewarding and fun
- You set higher expectations from yourself and others, and build that into the culture
- Helps the team learn to deal with healthy conflict in safe doses
- As the agent of change, you get to proactively educate Executives on why the change is good, and show them you perceived the need before they asked you to. They may appreciate it and support you.

And many more..

Personality Types

I am a fan of Personality Types Indicators. The reason I would consider it mandatory for every manager to learn their personality type, and also the ones for every person reporting to them where permitted by law, is that they indicate the preferred methods for that individual to communicate, perceive and analyze data both while calm and under stress. And we are all different.

In the learning to recognize and handle the differences, lies the gold mine for the team. As every personality type has its inherent strengths and weaknesses for the task at hand, any team with one or more unrepresented types runs the risk of fatal blind spots in its information processing and decision making.

The business benefit of supporting diversity in the workplace comes when that visible minority, with a different set of values and experiences gets to observe things most people around them never noticed, because "that's the way it is". And to the visible minority chap, well, that just doesn't suffice. So we hear instead: "really? Why would it be that way?"

I used to put my job on the line for ideas, then years later for projects, and now for the development of people (hence this book). I used to track data, then I tracked projects, and now I track potential in people. Today if some bean counter tells me they're concerned about overspending $10K on a $23M budget, I lose interest in the conversation. If you are trying to get my buy-in, you better understand me. Similarly if I am trying to get someone else's buy-in, I need to understand them. Know thyself. Know who you work for, and who you work with.

People grow through trauma, education, and experience. They mature with age. They grow especially through negative experiences, after due reflection. Big swingers include: cancer, death of a parent, the birth of unhealthy children, the inability to conceive, financial woes, breach of contract or trust, their experiences as a new immigrant, etc. These and more have ways to temper and shake the fabric that makes us – and help focus our reaction to future inputs. If you are serious about motivating people and making sure that your message lands on them, make sure you know what experiences or value system lens they filter the world with.

Make sure you tell them what works for you, too.

There are simple things you can do to train yourself into being more open minded for accepting or at least recognizing others' perspectives. Try this with a friend:

- Pick an argument, or a contentious topic (for e.g. capital punishment, legalization of abortion, existence of God, trial of minors as adults, castration of sex offenders, government's right to tap phones, employer's right to scan emails, right to strike of nurses, etc)

- Now pick a side. Defend it with vehemence - fight to win
- Now do the same for the opposite side.
- Look for a "third" side: pick a win/win mediation between the two previous views, for example. Get creative.
- Now go back to your first position: is it still so clear now? Do you feel it's still so black and white?
- How do you feel about the other side's validity as a possibility for someone's consideration, even if not yours?

In the process of attempting to win your side of the argument, did you take into consideration the thinking style of your opponent?

Peer Pressure and Group Culture

For many things that require saying, doing, and policing, I rely on peer pressure and group culture. It frees up my time considerably.

We have been exposed to peer pressure when a sibling got a higher mark on the report card, or when they produced a beautiful drawing, or drew praise from a parent. We have seen it among our friends when fashion changed and we were ahead of it, behind it, or just didn't participate. We experienced it when a coworker offered us cigarettes or a drink in public. We experienced it when someone hired around the same time as us, got promoted and we didn't.

We have all been subject to peer pressure, which is much more effective and pervasive than dealing with the manager of the day. Your manager evaluates you once a year, but you must face your peers every day.

A well functioning department requires key leaders aligned and supporting management. Also a critical mass of less influential folks bought into the direction and needs at hand. Then the outliers (and I classify them in terms of buy-in to the culture of the team, not agreement to decisions or methods), will in effect be faced with the choice of joining the department culture, or move on to other teams.

It's neither efficient nor effective for you to go into a department and say: "you fit, you don't". It's much more desirable for the team to evolve a culture and the constituent individuals to self select based on that culture. If you don't have influence over the key leaders, or a critical mass within the team, be aware that the conformance requirement will apply to you too!

Peer pressure and group culture is wonderful in that peers are in touch with an individual's performance and attitude, mood, more often and closely than a manager. As such they can provide the required feedback and influence without the manager being informed and long before the manager realizes there was a problem. This applies also when there is positive praise to be given! It may be the individual receives accolades from peers for accomplishments, before the manager is informed of them.

I think of the individual employees reporting to me and the culture of the department, as extensions of my persona. They allow for more leverage, better timing, and a smoother running department.

Stock Market Basics

Since so much of our business funding and investment decisions, bonuses, remunerations and communications seem slave to the stock price, it's important for managers to have a minimum of knowledge of stock pricing theory and practice.

Stock is issued by a company to raise funds with which to operate. It dilutes the ownership of this company, by allowing in most cases the owner of the stock to cast a vote during stock holder meetings, deciding on a number of issues at hand. It allows the owner of the majority of the available stock thusly to influence or control company policy.

If the stock pays a dividend, it returns money to the investor under the premise the money is best used by the investor than the company. Some companies choose to not pay dividends.

Stock price matters to the company because a second company may be able to buy its stock and through it gain control of the first company if the stock gets becomes affordable. Also if the stock becomes cheap, the issuing company may buy it back to regain control of its votes, and make each outstanding share more valuable.

Stock price should be a reflection of company worth and value – but it is not. Stock price moving up and down 20% in one year doesn't often reflect a significant increase or decrease in employees, buildings, salaries, assets, sales, or pretty much any other measurable debt or asset associated with the company. It is usually a reflection of the perception of the investors manipulating the stock price with their buying and selling of it, of whether the stock price they are tinkering with will be going up or down next. They do this while they and the company play a dance of information, guessing what financial targets the company should meet, and seeing whether it does.

The bottom, "real" price of a stock is the company's breakup value. If the company was cut up piece meal today, and money distributed to stock holders after debt is paid, how much would each share get paid? Usually much less than what the stock is trading at.

Stock Price

Let's build a formula for stock price:

Stock Price = Present Value of the Future (to the end of time) Dividends Generated by the Stock Certificate. The stock gives you the right to collect dividends when they are issued.

Now that we accept that companies are apt to go defunct long before the end of time, we further modify the definition with "plus the company's break up value". So now it looks like this:

Stock Price = Present Value of the Future (until dissolution of the company) Dividends Generated by the Stock Certificate + break up value of the company

There is more, but let's build up to it.

A stock provides two benefits to the stock holder. It provides a dividend if there is such a payout, and it provides a vote when one is required for a decision by the Company, if the stock is deemed to be a voting stock.

That is it!?

Let's look at the illustrative case, where a stock pays no dividend. It is worth as per theory: $0 + the break up value.

In practice, the stock price (not its value!) is further inflated by the hope that someone will want to buy it from you later, for more money still. This excuse for justifying buying into stock is known as "potential for capital gains", or "speculation".

Thus the revised, practical formula that bears closer semblance to what you see in the stock market, reads thusly:

Stock Price = Value of Stream of Dividends + Break Up Value + Investor Speculation

When someone tells me that the stock market lost one third of its value in a crash, I ought to have visions of an overnight fire burning one third of all companies like some apocalyptic cataclysm. Instead, I see the companies are operating just as well as they did the day before – though if some stocks crashed, other companies may look to buy controlling interest in them. Some executives may have lost a fortune in stock options, and the average investor will have hell to pay when his or her spouse hears they lost their savings for retirement, but other than that, it's not that big a deal. The companies themselves are unharmed. The factories didn't burn down. They have all the cash they had the day before. The customers didn't move to another planet. Their employees didn't all die overnight. Doesn't that give food for thought?

A crash is caused when a large enough number of speculators decide *en masse* to bail out of the game. When the market settles, the stock price has a smaller investor speculation component. We hear that "the market has had a correction, and is now more in line with the fundamentals".

The observations above earned me a lashing from a professor years ago, during one of my Advanced Finance courses. She was adamant that stock price reflected value, I countered it was mostly gambling. I remain unconvinced.

Public companies address the stock market need of having executives concern themselves with the future price of the stock by tying significant executive compensation to stock price. The pressures and temptation facing stock vested executives to make decisions to positively affect stock price in the short term, even if they could hurt the company's ability to thrive in the long term, must be enormous.

Your problem as a manager and leader: the vast majority of your employees don't get paid with stock, unlike your executives – so they don't really care about it. Your customers don't care about the value of your stock either. Making employee and product line decisions grounded on stock market optics is extremely dangerous to the long term health of a company. You are caught in between the executive and your people; they're both nervous and they're both right.

You have no chance to solve the above problem. I gave you the background I did so you'd at least understand it. Don't tilt at windmills; the problem is bigger than you.

Beating Las Vegas

If you were managing a professional sports team, you would you measure your achievements by comparing between the numbers in the "Win" column and the numbers in the "Lost" column.

However you know that for most sports there exist betting odds. For example: If Team A is supposed to beat Team B by 5 points, and "only" win by 4 points, a bet in Team A's favor "lost", and a bet in Team B's favor, "won". Thus we have the gambler's query: "how did the team do *against the odds*?"

The stock market has become this. A company and the speculators betting on its stock, play an information dance where each other's expectations (the odds for the bet) are set. For example: "the street (speculators) expects company X to announce a 3rd quarter profit of 45 cents per share". The company then sees the stock go up, flat, or down depending on their result against this projected number.

But this has little to do with whether the company is beating competitors, gaining market share, investing in innovative products, has a loyal and motivated workforce, etc. It is not a "win or loss". It is a result against the street bet. If professional sport teams worked as the companies in the stock market, we would see coaches employed and championships earned by teams who consistently beat the Las Vegas odds irrespective of whether the games they played were won or lost in the end.

I encourage you to read "*The Deming Management Method*" by Mary Walton. Handle customers and your team to the best of your abilities. Such things stand the test of time.

Balance Sheet Fundamentals

There are a few concepts you must be conversant in, namely: assets, liability (debt), owner equity, return on investment, cash, bankruptcy, revenue, return on assets, gross margin, etc. These concepts must be a permanent constituent of your tool bag, because this is how both executives who decide the company's future, and the investment analysts that send the stock price up and down, measure the health of your business.

I'll group these in digestible chunks in the following sections, but let's start with the very basics:

Revenue is sales, the money that comes into your business. You want this number to go up year over year (YoY), quarter to quarter (a year is divided into four quarters, of three months each), and in the quarter you just finished as compared to the same quarter the previous year. Realize that some quarters are more influential than others – you wouldn't compare the Christmas sales quarter of a toy manufacturer to the Summer one, but the Christmas sales one for the past three years could give you a meaningful trend you can act on.

Profit is the money you have left from the sales after you paid your expenses to make these sales and other costs of running your company. As profit grows, so does your company.

Cash is the money belonging to you, filling your pockets. It's what lets you pay for stuff you need to pay for now, without borrowing. It gives power, flexibility, and freedom of choice. Not having cash, or being illiquid, leads to bankruptcy. If you have very valuable buildings but cannot pay your workers, they don't come to work anymore. Your business shuts down. Your business will track both the health of the cash level appropriate to your industry, as well as the trend of its growth or decline.

Asset, Liability, Owner Equity

The company's balance sheet is its proof of financial health. Let's look at it using a simple house ownership example:

Let's pretend that you live in a house valued at $300,000. You owe a $200,000 mortgage on it to the bank, at 5% interest.

In financial terms, your house is a $300,000 asset. Your mortgage is a $200,000 liability, leaving you with $300,000 - $200,000 = $100,000 of equity.

ASSET = LIABILITY + OWNER EQUITY

What happens when your house goes up in value to $550,000?

Liability didn't change, so our formula would suggest that you are now sitting on $350,000 in equity.

This is a big deal, if you want to get a loan from the bank for something else, for e.g. to buy a car. The bank looks into your equity, and figures you can borrow money, incurring a greater liability. Maybe your equity is so huge that you can borrow enough to get a down payment for a second house.

However if the real estate market collapses, and your house is now valued at $150,000, the $200,000 mortgage implies your equity is $ -50,000. Negative! The bank then calls you and asks you to pay off some of the mortgage so that your debt is back to being less than the value of the house. You owe more than the house is worth, and that is not good for whoever lent you money. If you walk away from the house, they will not get their money back. (For the curious, this analogy also explains what happens during a *margin call*)

The Power of Debt Leveraging, and Depreciation

Let's pretend there is a car for purchase using debt financing (loan). The car costs $40,000, and interest rate is 10% for ease of calculations.

I could wait until I have $40,000 in cash but that may take a while. What about a loan, so I can drive the car today?

As a consumer with no tax deductions on my interest loan, buying the $40,000 car completely on debt financing would cost me $4,000 in interest payments each year.

On the other hand, a company's business expense is tax deductible. They would claim the same $4,000 as a business expense, and this would lower their taxes. In the end, maybe the real expense for them would be $2,000 or so. Thus I need to spend $4,000 as a consumer to afford a $40,000 car, while a company only needs to spend $2,000 for the same privilege.

As a consumer, I notice my car becomes less and less valuable each subsequent year. It gets worn out. The company notices it too, but calls it depreciation. Depreciation is also a business expense, which again lowers its taxes. Pretty soon the consumer realizes a company can get a car pretty much for free. Governments let this happen because companies this way buy lots of stuff, driving up need (demand) to produce more stuff for other companies, that in turn creates jobs and "feeds the economy". The government gets its tax money from the employees, as they don't have deductions to hide behind. That is why companies may stop paying for their taxes sometime in the first couple of months of the year, while the employees may take until June or later depending on the country's tax rates. This incentive program is also known as "corporate welfare", a surprisingly socialist setup for corporations used to maintain a capitalist system functioning. Sorry for the digression, but the observation is funny to me and far too few have figured it out.

Companies can procure more assets to achieve desired goals than consumers due to the power of debt financing. Companies benefit thus by borrowing relatively cheap money to invest this money on projects that hopefully expand the business. These projects, as investments, carry with them depreciation and other expenses that in turn lower taxes even more. It's not a money making machine – but it comes close.

Of course debt must be serviced. Even the money making machine requires food. That food is cash and you need a minimum of it to keep everything running smoothly. If a company uses all its cash to pay regular interest payments, and at some point cash stops flowing in, the volume of the interest payments will deplete the cash reserves and send a company into bankruptcy. You could own six factories, all running on loans from someone else's money, but if your cash on hand can't cover interest payments on your debt, electricity bills and payroll, you will go bankrupt and your assets sold off to pay creditors.

Liability covered in the earlier section, isn't just about loans. If you have to pay your employees, you have a debt obligation too. If you have to pay your suppliers for raw materials, you have debt obligations there also. Some debt is variable – you could choose to not borrow money, postpone expansion or purchase of capital for a few months. However, you can't postpone payroll, electricity, and rent.

Return on Investment and Return on Assets

Managers have finite resources to invest, and a myriad of investment opportunities to choose from. Return on Investment (ROI) is a tool to help make decisions on where to spend the next dollar.

Many companies have a minimum bar that must be met before an investment is considered at all. For example, you may hear of a 10X (ten times) ROI. It basically says that you must demonstrate that $1,000 spent on your budget for the purpose you specify, needs to directly lead to $10,000 in payoff. $10,000 / $1,000 = 10X. If you cannot demonstrate this, then don't bother asking for the money.

Another way is to compare between the various potential investments that made the 10X cut above. Thus sometimes (not always, due to mitigating strategic considerations) the business case with the highest promise of ROI will secure the funding. Also sometimes companies look at how quickly they would get their initial investment money back, to differentiate between investments that pay off about the same. You'll then hear of IRR (Internal Rate of Return).

Similar to this concept, is Return on Assets (ROA). If you own a few buildings and with them generate an income, you have a lower ROA than your competitor who makes the same revenue stream by using employees who work from home, and thus foregoes the expense of having dedicated offices.

Cash Flow

Cash is a very important measure of the short term health of the company. Cash can be used to be able to purchase something very quickly, without incurring debilitating debt or having to beg someone for a loan.

Cash flow is important in that you need to make sure the cash coming into your business needs to be equal or greater than the cash going out. If you're paying cash, and receiving "I owe you" notes, you will look good on paper by way of assets and liabilities, but won't be able to pay your phone bill.

Large companies like sitting on reasonable amounts of cash to buy smaller companies, or buy back stock (this raises the Earnings per Share ratio analysts track even when earnings are flat, by decreasing the number of shares we divide the earnings into). Cash is a wonderful thing to seize opportunities in the short term.

You must be careful that you don't look at cash figures too naively. For example, which company is in a stronger cash position below?

1. Company A, with $100 in Cash, and $50 in Debt
2. Company B, with $50 in Cash, and $0 in Debt?

A company can borrow money just before declaring its cash position. Cash is thus known as a "point in time" measurement. Maybe the two companies above are the same company, a day before and after securing a loan of $50. This little optical game is played quite a bit, and the company will disclose it in the small print within its Annual Report.

Point in Time Measurements

I identified Cash as a point in time measurement because it is something a company can change quickly and from it, I don't have a strong feeling for the health of the company. Of course if a company consistently is sitting on a Billion in cash, then fine, this is a good thing. But I want to see debt measurements as well before I pass judgment on its health.

Similarly, I am weary of Earning Per Share (EPS) movements, without first seeing if the company is buying back stock. Many companies buy back stock so the EPS number looks better. If you don't look in the annual report to see if (and how much) stock is being bought back, how do you assess an improvement (increase) in EPS?

Revenue, Profit, and Gross Margin

Revenue is your sales.

Gross Margin is your sales minus the expenses you incurred to achieve these sales.

Profit is what is left of your revenue after every expense is deducted, including expenses that had nothing to do with the generation of the revenue.

You pay taxes on your profit.

Accounting Rules

It is very easy to end up in an apple to orange comparison between companies, depending on how you calculate figures.   For example:

1. Company A declares income when the ink is signed on a contract, listing the income under Accounts Receivable (asset)
2. Company B declares income only when the payment is made for its product, in cash (asset).

Both of these are valid, but very different.   The difference is mostly in the timing. If your company does a huge amount of sales in December, for a year-end reporting bonanza, but the stuff sold won't be delivered and paid for until January, did your company have a good year this year, or a good start next year? (Let's ignore for now whether it's even legal to be able to choose how to report this, in your country).

This simple example affects a number of measurements: EPS (by having differences on when to declare earnings), ROI (same reason), to name two.

Is Accounts Receivable "as good as cash"?

Let's say the terms of payment were: 30% with the order, 50% upon delivery, and 20% within 30 days of delivery. When do you take credit for the money coming your way?

It's interesting that you want to declare all money coming to you as soon as possible, to get bonuses, promotions, wonderful reviews and increased stock price. But would you pay taxes on money that hasn't physically found its way into your bank account? Remember the government wants money too, and they own the jails ☺

To protect investors from questionable reporting, and companies and the government from each other, many countries have a set of accounting principles that are to be followed in a consistent manner by all companies.   If the company for any reason changes the style or nature of its reporting, or has to change the numbers due to some extraordinary event, it must disclose this information and rationale in the "Notes to the

Financial Statements". These provide a wealth of information for the investors who take the time, and I strongly urge you look up the annual report of any company you like, and comb through the Notes.

The company must always disclose what it says and does, and penalties are stiff when it doesn't. It also must be audited to ensure it did what it did. It can change its practices as it deems fit, but must tell you when it did so, and often times, why.

Annual Reports

All publicly traded companies must make available copies of their annual report for the asking. And they're free! They contain a wealth of information on the financial health of the company, a declaration of its year, and where it thinks the business is going next.

These reports normally disclose balance sheet comparisons to previous years so you can see trends, and contain the Notes that explain changes in accounting practices leading to changes in the numerical data that could otherwise mislead you.

When I dabbled in investments, I would call all the banks in the Financial Sector I cared about, and ask for all their Annual Reports. Then I would open all of them, and compare.

Sometimes I would get the reports of partner companies, sometimes competitors, sometimes from sectors who supplied other sectors. It's fascinating stuff, how a company explains how things went and how they'll go next. Especially if you keep a prior report and then you read how predictions went, and what explanations are offered for it. It's free and educational. Companies spend lots of money preparing these reports, and they're written according to strict rules. Get a few, and learn – especially read the one for your company, and your competitors, and customers!

Statistics

You can prove anything you like with numbers, but it would be good if you could understand them to present or digest data properly. The following are key:

Mean, or Average

Take a group of numbers. Count them. Sum them up, and divide by the count. You now have the average. So the average between these numbers {2, 4, 6, 8}, would be the sum of the numbers 2 + 4 + 6 + 8 divided by the count of numbers, namely 4. 20 / 4 = 5. The mean or average of this group of numbers is 5.

Standard Deviation

This extremely important measurement tells you how closely grouped your numbers are, within a set. Thus you expect that most of the numbers in a set of numbers are to be within more or less three standard deviations from the mean. Only two thirds of the numbers would be found within plus or minus one standard deviation from the mean. So if I told you that for a group of numbers that I won't be showing you, the mean is 47 and the standard deviation is 3, you would know that 2/3 of the numbers would be found to be plus or minus one standard deviation from the mean. Thus 47 +/- 3, or between 44 and 50. And nearly all of the numbers would be found between 3 standard deviations from the mean, or +/- 9. Thus they are found between 38 and 56.

In order to decrease the standard deviation, thus increasing your accuracy, you usually would need to increase your sample size – that is, gather more data. That's why life insurance salesmen don't tell you "your premium is $X, give or take $2,000". They tell you that your premium is $X, exactly. Of course they have no idea when you will die, exactly, but they have so much data showing when everyone else has died already and why, that they can give you in confidence your very own exact quote. Everyone else getting a quote, in aggregate, will allow them to do the payouts they are obliged to, and make a profit in addition. According to statistics, with a large enough population, if you don't die when you're supposed to, someone else will do the dying for you. Thus the insurance company feels quite comfortable giving you a quote.

P Values and Confidence Intervals

You will hear during election time, of polls that are valid within 5%, 19 times out of 20. That is also known as a "P Value of 5". It means this in layman's terms:

We don't know who is going to win exactly or precisely. However, based on how we did the survey (polling as many people as we did, and as randomly as possible), if we were to conduct the survey 20 times instead of just the one time we did, we would be confident the result would be this number (whatever they say), give or take 5% up or down from what we said, 19 times out of the 20.

So it's not a crystal ball, but as far as statistics is concerned, it is pretty close.

Margin of Error

One key piece of data I see ignored that drives me crazy, is the margin of error in a customer survey. I've had to deal with this more than once, myself:

"The customer satisfaction result this year, for product X, is 82%. Last year, it was 84%! Please explain why the drop? Show us a plan to get to 85% next year".

When I come across this, my first question is: "Please tell me what is the margin of error for this survey?" Let's pretend that is what it was +/- 3%, for illustrative purposes.

Thus the original statement could have been rewritten as: we polled the customers for their satisfaction, and our survey says that the results are between 79% (82 – 3) and 85% (82 + 3). The number you're asked to hit, 85%, is already within our range. If you wanted a lower +/- margin of error, you need to spend more money on a wider reaching survey (accuracy increases with sample size). But with the margin of error of +/- 3%, or a total spread of 6 %, all numbers within the 79%-85% range are equivalent for your purposes.

So, to answer the original question:

Last year, it was 84%! Please explain why the drop? *The data does not indicate a drop.*

Show us a plan to get to 85% next year? *We're there already.*

If your manager isn't willing to learn the above basic lesson in statistics, or (more likely) works for someone who is determined to show they are doing something whether the data makes sense or not, get ready to be told to make up a deck of charts explaining the drop and what you will do to get to 85% next year. Don't despair; it happens to a lot of people. We can't all work for smart managers and leaders. Don't begrudge your taxes being spent on an improving educational system; you're a victim of the underinvestment of your forefathers.

Accuracy vs. Precision

Let's look at this illustrative example:

We know for a fact that the bottle we hold in our hands holds exactly 500 ml of liquid. We give this bottle to three of our employees, and ask them to measure how much liquid is in the bottle. We get back

1. 498 ml
2. 502.3 ml
3. 497.38 ml

Which employee was most accurate? Which employee was most precise?

Employee 1 was most accurate, because his measurement was closest to the true 500 ml. He only missed by 2ml.

Employee 3 was most precise, for his answer was to two decimal places. Regrettably it was also the most inaccurate response; he missed by 2.62ml (Employee 2 missed by 2.3 ml).

People, Product, Process

Your job is about leading people to create something of value, in the most efficient and effective way possible. It's that simple, and that hard. But it's fun and meaningful, too!

Proud, valued and motivated people will make sure the Product ends up just right because it is the tangible reflection of their effort and self worth. They will tackle Process because they would see it as the way to minimize waste and improve the quality of their work experience. And these people will end up seeing more than you in the details that affect day to day work for two reasons: they are closer to it, and there are more of them. That frees you up to focus on the bigger picture, and the future.

You are required to set the direction or goal, or at least influence the decision on what Product to work on, and why. How to market it, position it, price it, what channels to use to sell it. What features or capabilities it ought to have. How it will be maintained, serviced, and what warranty makes sense.

The Process is the part of the equation that lets you decide how you want your resources spent. Do you want to spend more resources up front in planning, or is your organization better suited or biased towards more testing? Do you want to do most of the testing before the customer sees the product, or do you show them the product many times along the way and make modifications when the customer changes their mind?

People is *who*, Product is *what*, and Process is *how*. Respect all three, resisting the urge to make one more important than the rest.

Not all teams will have each leg of the tripod at the same height, so it's up to you to make them so. What is the point of getting the best surgeons in the world in a room, and then hand them toothpicks for the operation? Of what use is a scalpel in the hands of an accountant, for that same operation? And would you feel good about the result if you had a surgeon, the scalpel, but they didn't know the procedure for the particular operation required?

Be aware of your own preferences and blind spots. It is likely that you will focus on one of the three, and do it competently either because you're good at it or interested in it. It is likely also that you will focus on another, because it's the one your boss cares about. And the third, which you either are uncomfortable with or you don't normally think about, you leave in the hands of Fate. That one may come back to haunt you.

The Power of Denial

The concept of Denial is borrowed from Psychology. It is a defense mechanism where our brain refuses to accept reality, data, thoughts, feelings, because they hurt! We can't deal with the pain! Or at least, we don't think we can. Perhaps we are unaware that we do this. Whether we're aware of it or (usually) not, we still make decisions based on the thoughts we have and the data we perceive; the problem is that both are flawed if we filtered reality through our denial.

Your own personal denial as a leader, of
- The need to change
- Incoming danger
- Opportunities on the table
- Bias of your decisions
- Bias of your filtering input
- Your character flaws
- Gaps in your skills and experience
- And lots more

Puts you and your team at risk.

Can you recognize the truth? Can you handle the truth?

University is supposed to train us how to think. That may be, but in many cases it teaches us to get to the right textbook answer, and experimental science often falls into the trap of discarding data that doesn't fit a hypothesis, support what was discovered by those who went before you. It's hard to prove the Earth is not flat, when everyone else knows it is flat already, right? And yet everyone knew that as ships sailed further away from them, the bottoms disappeared before the masts. Do you discard valid data that doesn't fit your hypothesis, and then use your tremendous mental faculty to logically think your way into a completely defensible and ironclad wrong conclusion ready to withstand the test of time? Once you do, do you threaten to burn people at the stake when they openly disagree with you?

I have seen denial applied in damaging ways in the workplace. Not knowing when to kill a project isn't always a sign of cowardice or fear of admitting failure. Sometimes it is just denial, we won't admit just how out of hand and unsalvageable this has gotten – because we just can't see it while we're inside it!

Sometimes we go on denial on an employee we're trying to save from firing. They won't make it; we know they won't make it... though maybe if we give them another chance?

Some employees (and managers, leaders do this too) refuse feedback that won't validate their self image. For e.g.: someone wants to be a manager, though you tell them this can't happen while they don't like managers and don't value working with people. They argue with you, and later on they come back with: "a year has passed, can I be a manager now?" They thought that a year later you would change your mind? The point of the year was for them to demonstrate that they grew up! They really didn't believe you that they had to improve something – they thought instead that you had to improve your judgment. That's denial. See you next year!

Denial is insidious and pervasive. It is about self image, what we want to see and believe in, irrespective of what everyone else would perceive to be reality. Consider that if you validate people around you, they won't be relying so much on denial to prop up their self image. If you have a life partner providing you with unconditional love and support, you won't have to lie to yourself about life, either. You will be more receptive to feedback. To tackle someone's denial, you must first earn their trust. They have to lower their guard to be able to open their mind to your input and ideas. And the same goes for you in getting feedback from them.

Sunk Cost

The management concept we borrow from Economics Theory, is that money you spent to date ought not to influence the decision as to whether or not to continue spending – if the money is already gone. It is a "sunk" cost. You can't decide whether to spend it or not, it's been spent already. Decide what to do with your remaining money only.

Of course your own manager may have strong opinions on what do to with and to you regarding your cavalier attitude towards money already spent, if you were to develop such an attitude. But in spite of angry sponsors, money already spent is the proverbial water under the bridge – hope it returns you profits, but that investment decision is gone. This concept works in several ways, so let's illustrate some:

You're on the way home from the subway, having bought two tickets to a show. When you get home and take off your jacket, you realize to your horror, that you lost your tickets!! Should you buy a replacement pair and go to the show anyway, or do you tell yourself that you already bought them once, so you don't go to the show? Assuming you can afford a second pair of tickets, the concept of sunk cost would tell you that nothing changed from your decision to buy the 1st pair, to the 2nd pair. It was good to buy the 1st pair, and for all the same reasons it's just as good to buy the 2nd pair. Enjoy the show!

However, many people see the cost of the 1st pair as part of the decision for the 2nd pair. In effect, they see the 2nd pair of tickets as costing double! Sure, you will have spent twice the money in the end, but the 1st half is already spent. The 2nd pair shouldn't be penalized, the cost inflated by the 1st pair. Sunk cost says: go buy the tickets. Whether you lost the original tickets or donated their value to charity is irrelevant to the purchase decision of the 2nd pair.

Another common scenario concerns the cost overrun. Say we're building a nuclear power plant, and halfway through the project, we're 40% over cost. That is terrible, to be sure, and someone may get punished for it. However, is that overrun reason enough to stop work on the project? Sunk cost says that we should look at what there is to be gained from completing the project (affordable electrical capacity, customer service, environmental considerations from the completed result). It doesn't matter what was spent to date, that money is gone. The point is, are we poised to get a worthwhile benefit that is better than the extra money to be spent? Evaluations and accountants will demand and obtain a reckoning of the total expense vs. original budget, but that is separate from the decision required to finish or stop the construction of the power plant.

Casinos get rich by playing to the gambler's inability to objectively consider sunk cost. The losing gambler often times decides to keep playing when his money runs out, and will seek out a loan to "get my money back". What? You gambled, lost, and presumably obtained your payoff by way of entertainment. What do you mean, "lend me money so I can get money back"? If that was the goal, stay at home, and you keep the money you had to begin with, without risking mine as well. Or if they still have some money, they may say "I lost $X, I need to keep going". No, whatever you lost has nothing to do with whether you're to keep going, or not. Your decision to keep going is all about whether you figure the money you're about to gamble, provides a return in terms of money or entertainment, or stress, that makes it worthwhile. It is a future looking decision, not a past focus decision.

It applies to the workplace too: "I invested so many years into this company" (so?); "it may get better" (Through fate or an act of God? What do you need from this company?)

If you're the parent of a student looking to quit a University Degree a year from graduation, you could say "you spent X years already, finish it". If the student is versed in sunk cost, try instead: "you probably can't imagine one more day in that field, but think; you're just one year away from a University Degree! That's nothing! There is not a degree in the world that is attainable in just one year! What a payoff for so little future effort!"

The common thread in all of the above is the requirement to remove from your decision of present and future benefits and costs, what you spent on the topic already. Because what you did is not relevant to what you are after, only what you're willing to do for it, now and in the future.

Changing Employee Demographics and Company Communication

As the generations march through the workplace, changes are evident that are not just due to legislation or immigration, or even culture.

The big changes are generational. We work for senior leaders in their 60s raised in a peer group where the choices were to lead or obey; we manage as fairly independent members of a generation in their 40s that won't take guidance from anyone we don't respect; we manage a bunch of kids in their 20s that are used to and demand constant stimulation and gratification, and have no use for advice they can't read in a blog.

Add to that the natural differences in the relative perception of time horizons experienced by the representatives of each generation, plus the relative intolerance to discomfort from the new blood, and you now see yourself caught in quite the corporate sandwich. Your boss tells you to do more with less, you feel you have to try to do different things because you know your job better than your boss, and your employee has placed your company on three year probation because that is pretty much how much discomfort he or she is willing to endure in an unpleasant environment.

Buy-in is more important than ever. If you base your communication on what you find compelling, you may be heard and ignored. If you can phrase it around what resonates for them, you may be listened to and have an impact.

The corporate sandwich the manager is under these days is exemplified most clearly in communication from Executives and HR. Managers look at these communications and shudder at the thought of delivering the message and how it may train-wreck the fragile team's morale and productivity with it. Morale and productivity they worked so hard and diligently to build up. You will hear managers complain: "my people won't buy this" and they're worried and scared of their job as messengers.

It is your job as manager to find out why the communication was required in the first place, and translate this into a message acceptable by your people because you know them best. You own the communication to your team. Ask upwards, explain downwards. If you don't add value both ways, the two generation gap you're caught up in, will hurt you.

Transparency

It's tempting to decline ownership for corporate communication that you're expected to deliver, but you don't believe in yourself. However it is part of your job to stand behind said communication as if it were your own.

You may be told to say to your people that they're well paid, though your employer doesn't pay the bulk of your team as well as the competition. Or you may be told to get your people to work harder, and not claim overtime, because they ought to be grateful they have jobs at all (but you know they're marketable). You may be told there is belt tightening because we're into rough times (but you know that headquarters is fat, and a quick internet query of your firm's officers under *Yahoo Insider firm-name* shows so many of them cashing in millions in stock). You may be told to communicate the company fell far short of its yearly goals in revenue and profit, but you know that this is in part due to the goals being set arbitrarily high, to minimize the bonus payable. After all, the stock analysts were told we're doing better than last year, right?

Your job is to present what you're told to present. However you're creative, resourceful, and quite the leader in your own right – nothing stops you from putting your own spin. So for example, you could tell your people that we're well paid vs. the offshore employees, and that labor arbitrage pressure continues for the short term. Let's not make the gap bigger else we lose more jobs. You can also tell your folks what they need to do to make themselves more marketable, so you have a better business case in your hand to get more money to retain your people. You can't make your company's pay more competitive, but nothing stops you from justifying more money for your team. In the case of stock analysts being told we're great, while your employees are being told we stink, sooner or later the company will have to address it. When the business or the economy turns around, your company will lose talent to the competition, and then salaries will have to become more competitive. And so it goes. So have patience. The gaps in common sense won't last long.

Understand that your job is to toe the company line in the best manner you see fit to your particular team, since you know your team best.

Rest assured that however dysfunctional the message you're asked to convey, the marketplace forces (customers, competitors, labor, investors, government and the law) will eventually smooth out anything truly out of whack. Meanwhile challenge yourself to smooth out the rough edges. If you agree with the company's goals and are in touch with your employees' needs, then you ought to be able to find a common ground. Surely you can put a temporary positive spin on pretty much anything that comes across your desk, while you look for better longer term solutions.

In the rare situation where you're completely stupefied by the message you're asked to deliver, you can always put your stupidity to work. Thus, you can send an email to HR saying: "*I want to do my very best presenting the message you asked me to present, in the best possible light. However I have not been able to figure out the proper answer to the following questions I expect from my team, and I feel I can't proceed until you have helped me prepare for them. Please help me, by providing me with the answers, or other suitable guidance?*" Then list the obvious questions, and make sure your manager is informed that you have asked them. Odds are that what is on your mind is on the minds of many other managers and the answers will benefit the company as a whole. You don't need to blindly follow, and you ought not to blindly roadblock – it is much better to influence the people making the requests, and be part of the larger team for the common good. After all, we all have the same goal, namely creating an ever more successful company and better working environment for us all.

Having said all of the above, many times you are asked to communicate things that you do believe in, but you can't disclose the facts behind them to a group of employees who will question your intelligence. So you will help communicate the killing of a project, but you can't talk about the new secret project that will be funded with the money. Then you need to take the arrows on behalf of the long term health of the organization.

Tilting at Windmills

I have wasted more energy than I care to remember aggravated at things that offended me or hurt the work environment I was trying to create for myself and my teams. However, I have also noticed that with every rung I climbed up the corporate ladder, I was exposed to more decisions with sensitive data which necessitated my communication of partially explained decisions. These decisions I hoped would be accepted on faith from me because people ought to trust my unimpeachable character and integrity. What about those employees who didn't know me?

This taught me that while there are instances where some decisions are visibly questionable and perhaps incorrect, there are also instances where they are absolutely appropriate but the data to prove this, cannot be shared. In those situations, I left myself rightfully open to abuse by those below me.

With this new insight, I wondered if perhaps I had been unfair and unjust on occasion, when I mentally derided some of my managers for doing or saying things that on the surface were not defensible. *Walk a mile in someone else's shoes*, the saying goes. Perhaps we ought to give people the benefit of the doubt more than we do, to rightly hope that it will be given to us?

As years passed and my experience grew, I lost a lot of my tolerance for people who tilted at windmills. I trained my folks to complain for short whiles if it felt good, for longer only if they saw the complaining as useful brainstorming and identification of something they would immediately get to personally influence and fix. But complaining for the sake of complaining? No. There is no point complaining if nothing will come of it. That brings everyone down, lowers everyone's morale and productivity. If you won't be spurned to action or change, then accept it and move on to something else.

It's not easy to attain the discipline required to stop complaining about dumb things, but selecting which battles to fight, and which to not, is a necessary skill for your tool bag. Not tilting at windmills also saves your energy for expenditure when you need it later, when it will make a difference. It also lets you train yourself to focus on where you get the biggest bang for the buck. That way you can also increase your chances of making progress, and having successes to show for your energy and effort. It will also help you surround yourself with "can do", positive people.

What Makes a Successful Employee

It is my personal opinion and conviction that what separates the top from the bottom in an otherwise bright and wonderful group of employees is the *individual willingness of an employee to make an impact.* I have stated this at my area meetings for years.

Whether they are successful at it depends on a number of factors, generally. Proactive employees do better than reactive ones. Leaders fare better than followers. Better dressed may do better than shabbily dressed, well spoken better than those with foul language, etc. But the willingness to make an impact, I assert, divides the chaff from the wheat. People willing to make an impact will manage to get things done, somehow. And you will reward them for it, if you want them to keep doing it for you.

Note that I am defining success from the point of view of the employer. Namely did the employee keep rising through the ranks, does he or she continue to display ambition, do they keep meriting salary increases, etc.

The employee definition of success may be different from the company's. They may define it as a proper work / life balance, or happiness, or a window office, salary, or a title. Flexible working hours while juggling single parenthood. Perhaps they want job security, or ongoing opportunities for formal education and retooling. You have what it takes to marry the two successes, so both the company and the employee get what they want.

In the end, success is all about "job fit". If the job requires you to do well the stuff you are naturally gifted to do, that you love to do, that you are good at, then you're being paid to be yourself. Wonderful! But most jobs don't fit us like so many perfect gloves, so the willingness to make an impact - our Attitude - is the main determinant. You will select your friends, coworkers, partners and people working for you, on their willingness to contribute to your friendship, workplace, home, projects. Some people just get the job done, no matter what skills and experience they brought to the table. You rarely know what academic training anyone has who works with you, and you likely have neither clue nor interest on what marks were obtained while in school. But you care very much whether they will contribute, and whether you can rely on them. Are they, like you, willing to make this a winning team no matter what? Will they leave their mark? Will they want their name associated with the end product, when the customer buys it?

Conflict Management

Conflict, namely two opposite or disparate viewpoints clashing on common ground, may be healthy or unhealthy. Healthy conflict, such as realizing early in the project that the design has a flaw, is a good thing. Unhealthy conflict, such as undermining an individual's contribution because they got their job through perceived nepotism, is not.

The big problem with conflict management is that by and large we're not good at it. An eminence in the medical and psychiatric community once explained to me that under stress, our bodies are governed by something inside our skulls approximately the size of an acorn that is limiting our options to a primordial choice between Fight or Flight. This is what helped our cave dwelling ancestors survive when a bear showed up at the mouth of the cave, or showed interest in the deer just hunted. It takes 20 minutes to clear the adrenaline from our bloodstream and regain our orange size brain with so much more capacity for elegant solutions, once we remove ourselves from the stressful situation. When was the last time you were given 20 minutes to cool off after receiving really bad news in the workplace? When was the last time you gave yourself 20 minutes to ponder calmly on your response, when faced with a travesty? More often than not, you likely gave someone a piece of your mind instead or quickly fired off an email.

Assuming that we're in control of our ancestral inheritance of adrenalin and instinct, we still have not been trained to resolve conflict in a manner leading to win/win. Our society bombards us with winners and losers. We treat many interactions like the purchase of a used car. They are ripping us off, and we need to protect ourselves. If they agree to our position, we were too soft and got robbed, or the car was a lemon. Trust no-one.

In the workplace, we ought to be interested in win/win because we need to keep working with these people! You may rob or be robbed once, and that will be the last time this relationship will have been characterized by untapped potential and possibilities. Rebuilding trust takes years, after that. You may not even be given the chance, nor may you want to grant it.

I offer that there is no other way to preserve professional working relationships in the workplace, enabling required future cooperation and synergy, than a win/win conflict resolution. You don't have a choice. And even though the evaluation and rewards system at hand will pit you against others, your emotional intelligence better serve you to navigate a win/win solution lest the work environment become a hell to visit for too many days into the future. Projects come and go and are too soon forgotten along with the labors that went into them. The reputation you acquired as a coworker while achieving those results, sticks around. Do you want people to work for you? Try to go the extra distance? Do you want to surround yourself with professionals or bullies? Perfect your conflict management skills.

And when you just can't find a way to work with some people, trust that there are still ways around it. For example:

Once a manager I liked gave me the difficult task of showing I could work with an individual I found both incompetent as well as insufferable. So I thought long and hard on the problem. Fact: nothing this individual had ever done or said provided me with value. Fact: stuff communicated from this individual either annoyed me or made me upset. Solution: stop the communication from reaching me! I changed my email settings so that emails from said individual would be routed automatically to a trash folder that would be wiped out by the system in a fixed number of days. Wonder of wonders, upon my following evaluation many months later, my manager was overjoyed at my personal growth, how the relationship had improved, there was no visible conflict, etc. I've only done this to two people in two decades of professional work; proving that you can work with pretty much anyone.

Emotional Intelligence and the Value of NO

It is hard to deal successfully with conflict (meaning getting what you need while preserving long term relationships) if you're not on top of your impulses, your emotions, and those exhibited by your peers and counterparts.

We see this often dealing with our employees, and our immediate manager, when faced with how to say or receive that very important word: "NO".

"No" conveys disappointment, a temporary challenge to the relationship, opens the door to short term conflict, and reaffirms or sets a boundary. Children have difficulty processing the word "No" from a parent, though they have heard it so often that they learned it before "Yes". Many managers have difficulties hearing it also, and many employees have difficulties offering it. Some executives are physically incapable of processing a "No" directed at them. Their ears seem to function only immediately before and after that word. In the military, sometimes soldiers get shot by their own side as a reward for saying "No". It's heady stuff!

What is the value of "No" to the organization? It is tremendous, in my opinion:

- It allows whoever offers it, the opportunity to provide an alternate viewpoint on the same problem, perhaps even provide value and reasons the requestor had overlooked
- It allows whoever says it, the opportunity to disclose boundaries that existed all along, material to the health of the relationship
- It allows the relationship to redefine itself by acknowledging the limits of what can be done by it, today – perhaps these limits may be stretched by the now identified need for additional creativity, brainstorming, training, additional resources to the problem, or growth of skills and experience
- It helps prevent the requestor from booking an over commitment to external stakeholders or sponsors – saying "yes" when things can't be done, amounts to a

set up for failure right from the start. I would be very upset if someone said "yes" to me when I made a request, knowing full well it couldn't be done. It is professional negligence and breach of trust in our relationship. I want that person off my team!

- It immediately triggers the identification of the risks and associated mitigation plans that redefine the problem in such a way as to make a "yes" possible. Often times the requestor has a hidden agenda, reasons or flexibility that if disclosed, changes the parameters of the request enough to allow the doer to say "yes". For example, is the deadline driven by a customer commitment or was it just a stick in the ground because a deadline has to exist? Did we need this very complicated and high risk, extra feature? Or is the bulk of the low risk product good enough?
- "No" puts to the test and thus helps reaffirm the strength of the relationship, thus in a strong way contributing to the climate of the organization.
- It reaffirms to stakeholders and sponsors that indeed the area is working at capacity
- It allows for a fresh look at the area's current activities and priorities
- It allows for a reaffirmation that participants were hired for their intelligence, thought and value add to the organization – they have the opportunity if correct to prove they are experts, through the professional justification of their rejection

And so much more.

Differentiation, Fairness, Rewards

If everyone in your organization earns salaries determined strictly by accumulated years of service, what motivates you to do your job to the best of your abilities?

If you have a sense of entitlement to what you get just because you are who you are, who are you trying to please when you put in extra effort? Would you put in extra effort?

Do you really believe everyone works to the best of their abilities, if they get paid the same no matter what? If someone around them doesn't apply themselves, how do they react? If their peers work extremely hard, would they follow the example?

The Communist Farm System in place in the USSR years ago realized that production was suboptimal because the farmers were not motivated, rewarded for stretching themselves. Because overall production and influx of farm goods into the system was the ultimate goal, some communities allowed farmers to tend a relatively small plot of land after their communal work was done, with the understanding that the produce from these small plots would benefit the individual farmer alone. These tiny plots produced yields per acre much higher than those of the communal plots, because the individual farmers could see a correlation between their individual rewards and their individual labor. That is human nature.

You, me, and our employees - like the farmer - like and want to be individually recognized for our inherent goodness and uniqueness. We want everyone to do well, but we don't think it is fair that we get paid the same if we apply ourselves to different levels as our coworkers, or if we carry different levels of risk, responsibility. We expect that management recognize our uniqueness and efforts through a differentiation of our compensation from our peers. We don't need them to be put down, that gains us nothing and it is destructive. But we would like to be raised in relation to our contribution and efforts.

A manager's views on differentiation have a strong impact on the morale of the team, and provide tangible and consistent feedback to the employee in line with the progression of status reporting against agreed to goals, and assigned tasks. The communication on salary increases and how you justify their amount needs to be consistent with the message you provide come evaluation time. This is all connected in the employee's mind, and needs to be connected in yours.

We want to be rewarded for our efforts. The handling of the public recognition of efforts provided by one or more individuals is a powerful indicator of what behavior pleases management and is to be emulated. If the justification for said recognition is not clear, people will assume less than complimentary reasons as to why the award was granted, with a destructive effect to the organization, your perceived competence, and the individual who received it.

The Role of Human Resources (HR)

This varies from company to company, and there is no right answer. What are you to expect from them by way of support for your managerial duties?

There are a number of personnel related items that I expect:

- They can make the job offer to candidates I choose to hire, by use of a standard package reflecting company policy, introduction, and in adherence to the latest in labor law legislation
- They can be used as an alternative dispute resolution path if an employee has a strong disagreement with me, and they don't trust my own superior to be fair, empathic or competent
- They can enforce and safeguard company policy and its consistent interpretation to a wide set of managers throughout the company
- They can handle an employee's dismissal package
- They can get involved in benefits and their management
- They can contact other companies' HR teams to compare remuneration and benefits, practices so to ensure everyone is at the desired level of competitiveness within their industry
- They can handle interview bookings, communication with University Campus, job postings, Contracting Agencies, and provide a central point of contact with outside job seekers
- They can help recruit from other companies. Microsoft, in my experience, excels at this. So did Northern Telecom in the 1980s. Alas I've also interviewed with other companies where the people from HR who met with me were not qualified for the task at hand – and this reflected very poorly on my view of their company. I had an interview once with a chap from a public utility firm who was unable to pronounce or point out on a map, the city he expected me to move to if I joined his firm. Seriously!
- They compile and keep indicator data in terms of demographics and compensation that may help me make decisions about my teams in terms of composition or remuneration
- They may gain the departing employee's trust so we know as an area and company the reasons we lose talent. Whether brain drain to other countries, pervasive salary issues, perceived ceiling on opportunity for advancement, etc, these cumulative data over time may be of value to management or lead to the retuning of company policy – and is often available for the asking.

I once asked a trained and professionally certified HR person to tell me what her job was, in her view. I got: ***The primary job of HR is that the company is not successfully sued.***

That was a shocker! Was I naïve to assume anything else? She laughed at me.

HR's job is not to defend you or your employee during a grievance. It is to protect the company from harmful legal and media exposure. The lesson for you as the manager and leader is this: The best way around HR issues is to prevent them from happening in the first place through your good management, maintenance of open communication with your employees so problems get handled while they are still small, and expectations setting so that disappointments are minimized. I recommend you engage in activities aimed at building trust and a respectful, professional environment.

Dealing and Empathizing with Your Bosses

One of the huge determinants on your personal morale and job satisfaction is your immediate manager. The upside of this is that you could have a supportive manager who is a great personal coach, teaches you from his or her experience, is fair, provides you with what you need to get the job done, rewards and validates your achievements, provides professional constructive criticism... a joy of a human being to work for. Before you get too excited, keep in mind that such people comprise the exception rather than the rule. I have had two such managers thus far in my career. For the rest, you hope that they will be neutral and fair. Alas, sometimes you don't even get that.

You will find when you climb any number of rungs in the management ladder, that the people above you are surprisingly human, fallible, and insecure. They are not omniscient and omnipresent, or all mighty. Quite the contrary they screw up, often, and big. At best you could say that they are dedicated, driven, ambitious and resourceful. That they got lucky in that someone more powerful than them supported and recognized them early in their career, and they got hold of successful and visible projects. In some ways they are the pawns of fate, not much less than the girl who was born a princess and the one who was born in a slum. They were fortunate to be exposed to opportunities, and were smart enough to seize them, and fortunate enough to see their labor pay off. But this is not the stuff infallible leaders are made of. So don't think of them that way, and don't judge them so harshly. They are human, and if you learn to empathize with them, you will realize that they are not the enemy and they are not out to mess with you, normally. That mindset will immediately lower your frustration in your job, and since you won't be defensive around them, and you will listen, you will find they may lower their guard around you. You will both benefit from a better relationship.

Normally your boss (and the bosses above her) has likely a higher personal investment in the job than you. Likely has sacrificed more personal time, time with children, with friends, parents, than you – for a payoff that is likely dubious and temporary (we all retire from our jobs, even if it is by dying on the job). The boss may be insecure by how much longer her own boss will continue to see her growing experience as an asset worthy of the much higher pay and vacation benefits than would be paid to newly hired skilled workers into the company. Your boss is dealing with fears of obsolescence, loss of power bases, stress from company mergers and acquisitions, outsourcing, globalization, and all manner of changes seen and unforeseen. Plus she is vulnerable. It is very likely that removing her from her job will have no noticeable short term impact on the output of your area, and she knows this.

Your boss is used to making decisions without all the information or data required, but that doesn't make her infallible, or prescient. One day, she will make a colossal blunder, and there may be dire consequences. She is worried about her success, her career, her time until retirement, her marriage, her parents, her health, her teenage children, her role as a mother, etc. She may be starved for validation and affection. She may be sick and tired of never being able to show she is tired, stressed, or has a bad day. Your boss has much bigger problems in the workplace than you, and mistakes are more visible and carry worse penalties. The higher you are, the bigger the fall!

Does your boss really have the time and energy to go petty on you? Sure, some managers are attracted to the job because they get to be legal bullies of other people. But those small time punks aside, what does a manager gain from making your life hell and blocking your progress and success in your job? You are doing a job for them, so your failure is their failure, right?

I find that empathy with your manager is a required first step towards lowering the stress and frustration in your job. After all, odds are their headaches and yours, have much in common. And they're too busy with their problems to really go out of their way to make your life worse – if they do this, it is likely out of ignorance or their own failings. They are a human package of good and bad, after all.

I think how we phrase our thoughts has much to do with how our coworkers and our bosses react to us. Caught up in the heat of the moment, we may say:

"I suggest this idea because clearly the way we do things doesn't work, here is the data. So my idea is to do this instead, which makes things better because of ... " And we wait for them to agree, though in some cases we are expecting the boss to disagree as further proof that they are unsupportive idiots, and good effort is wasted in this job.

What would work much better is "I know we do this in such a manner today for the following good reasons, but that way we also leave this much gold on the table. I was curious as to your opinion on this idea I had, to get some of the gold. I would appreciate your insights on what maybe be bad about this idea too, that I just can't see from my point of view – it is likely I have a blind spot, you know how it is when someone gets excited about something".

The two conversations above build different environments and relationships. The first scenario says:

- It's about ME
- MY idea
- Your value add is to AGREE WITH ME
- You as a manager allowed this bad thing to go on for how long?

The second scenario says:

- I value what you have built and managed so far
- There is stuff out there we can all benefit from – an opportunity to make things even better
- I value your insights and experience, I invite you to be part of the solution

- I realize I don't have all the answers, but I am trying for some progress (some of the gold)
- I welcome feedback – where could I be going astray?   I value our relationship more than my ego; I am secure about myself already.
- I have enthusiasm – I am trying.   Share my energy.
- It's about the problem to be solved or the opportunity to be mined, not proving I am smarter than you.

It is hard for a manager to turn down good intentions and an offer of a positive and respectful relationship.   Do you have enough friends at work?   Can you have enough friends at work?

We all have what it takes to charm people.   All of us.   Smiles are free.   You don't have to pretend to like people, or to care about them if you don't.   But a professional behavior is a must.   Giving people the benefit of the doubt while they do a job you don't understand, that you have not done yourself and you can't prove you would do any better, makes common sense.   Stay away from dangerous tendencies to judge others in black and white terms, at best an indefensible course of action.   If you are good at what you do, your manager has the headache of keeping you happy in your job.   Help them help you.

You cannot control the inputs coming your way, but you can control how you react to them.   And no leader in charge of anything meaningful has a cushy job.   You'd want support and understanding, forgiveness and benefit of the doubt applied to you if you had your boss' job – do you extend them the same courtesy?   They probably get paid more than you, but you don't know what they sacrificed to make the extra money, nor if you would pay such a price in their shoes.   They may be saving you from having to do that job, yourself.   Be grateful that you have a boss.   They are worried about stuff you don't need to know, nor want to, until you're ready to.   Help them succeed.

Remember that how you treat your parents, is how your kids will one day treat you.   If your peers saw you undermine your manager, would they trust you when they become your manager?   And what have you taught them on what you deem proper behavior towards you, when you become their manager?

Career Growth and the Employee

One of the areas where the manager can provide tremendous value add, and the employee welcomes his or her involvement while both get the opportunity to engage in relationship building, is the area of employee career and skills development.

There is no substitute for this activity. It doesn't need to be formal, but it has to get done.

Goals vs. Ambition

First of all, you are required to educate the employee on the difference between Goals and Ambition. Goals are what you want. "I want to be Vice President", is a goal. It may not be a realistic goal, but that is not for you to judge. Goals, dreams, are valid by definition. Be supportive and encouraging when your employee tells you his or her goals.

Ambition is what you are willing to do to achieve your goal. For example: "to achieve my goal to become Vice President, I will go to night school and get my MBA. I will also work on high risk projects, and listen to a mentor that you will suggest for me. I want to list the top three things that in your opinion, my dear manager, get in the way of even better results from me. I will put plans in place within a month to tackle these failings, and you will provide me with an assessment in six months as to whether you see progress. I expect of myself that you won't recognize me in these three topics, by year end. I will go from amateur to expert! I will take on the mentoring of three more junior people to make them so good, I will be forced to constantly improve to keep them interested in what else they can learn from me. Company project managers will be driven to tears of gratitude when I am assigned to their projects. People will refuse to leave teams I manage, will in fact have to be forced out. I demand to receive immediate feedback of my failings, and I give you permission to punish me if I don't acknowledge your feedback, and show steps to correct it. My punishment will be skipping this year's bonus, and I give you permission to do so, here and in writing."

Clear?

Stress in employee relations will often time be traced back to the gap between goals and ambition, where naturally ambition falls far short of the goal. If you want to run your own convenience store, you better expect to work at least 60 hours a week. As a manager, when I hear a lofty goal, I applaud it and then ask: "how do you intend to get there"? Normally that tells me about their ambition. Too many times I hear "well if I stay doing this for a couple of years, eventually it will be my turn to be promoted". Then my coaching work begins in earnest.

Thus here is one more tool I use to assess and influence people's happiness, and indirectly, their productivity: by observing whether there is a lockstep match between goals and ambition, and doing something about it. Let's take an example from outside the workplace, namely a person who has been told by her doctor that she is overweight.

We could have an overweight person who has a goal to lose weight, and chooses to change her lifestyle to achieve it. Chances are high that this person will be happy while her ambition is in line with her goals, at every step in her journey, even during times when she achieves no progress whatsoever.

We could have an overweight person who has a goal to lose weight, but refuses to change her lifestyle to achieve this goal. This person will be quite unhappy and dissatisfied, as clothes, scales, doctors will remind her of her inability to attain her goal, even if her inertia is the main roadblock to progress.

We could have an overweight person who could lose the weight, but chooses the goal to accept herself as she is, and will buy whatever clothes flatter her figure and surround herself with friends who accept her as she is. Her ambition and her goal are in sync, and while she's not losing an ounce, she is perfectly happy. She has chosen to accept herself as she is, and thus set that as her goal. Her ambition supports her goals. She is overweight and happy.

We could have an overweight person who has the goal to lose weight and the ambition to pull it off, but for medical reasons can't lose the weight. The goal is unattainable. The person will be unhappy until she resets her goal to the realistic limitations of her metabolism and health, and focus her ambitions elsewhere.

In this simple illustration, happiness was attained when the individual either boosted her ambition to match her goals, or changed her goals to something that could be supported by her ambition, or changed her goals to what was realistic and re-channeled her ambitions elsewhere. The weight of the individual was not the determinant of happiness; keeping the gap between goals and ambition to a minimum, was.

The example has more to offer. You can influence people by aiming at their goals or their ambition. Doctors try to drive into you goals of weight loss, but they mostly are ineffective in their ability to have you embrace these goals unless they scare you into a fear of imminent death, heart disease, cancer, diabetes.

Weight loss clinics are much more sophisticated and successful. Your doctor will still be employed if you die from complications arising from excess weight, but weight loss clinics would go bankrupt if nobody would act on their message. They first bombard you with pressure and influence to set your goal at some level of weight loss, promising that it is an achievable goal by showing examples of success stories (never mind the small print saying the results are not typical), together with lots of help to boost your ambition (how wonderful you will look with new clothes, how it may improve your sex life, the yummy food you can eat guilt free while you lose weight, what celebrity you may like endorses it, etc). The weight loss companies know that the goal alone is insufficient – if it were, the doctors would have had enough of an impact already.   The most successful weight loss companies also tackle the minimal ambition of the individual by showing the goal is attainable without undue pain and suffering. Things look easy, we'll help you – so you'll give it a serious try.

In the workplace, one obvious way to increase people's ambitions is through the salary program, offering raises to those who try harder. Through the awards program, providing validation and recognition to those who exhibit behaviors management wants emulated, so others may have the ambition to copy them. Through promotions, feedback, pats-in-the-back, bigger offices, windows, company car, expense account, secretaries, lofty titles, etc. By showing successful and humane role models – if they can do it, and they have families, why not you? Etc.

Short Term vs. Long Term Goals

It is valuable to have the employee visualize themselves 1-2 years from now, and 5 years from now, or longer.   This takes a lot of time, and many people are afraid to share that vision, never mind face it in privacy and secrecy. They will be tremendously disappointed if you don't follow up.   They need to see you care – and trust me, you should. It makes you feel good and valuable, provides your employee with growth that benefits everyone, and builds a stronger relationship between you two. There's not a single detractor to this activity – though many managers ignore it.

Discovering long term goals is crucially important because they point to the optimal subset of short term goals and activities that should be tried next from where we are today.

Current Skills and Experience Inventory, and Gaps

From the preceding discussion on goals, you will naturally then list the things the employee is proficient at, and what needs improvement especially in terms of the requirements towards the achievement of the stated goals. Their goals, not yours for them! These gaps in skills and experience require tackling through formal education or on the job experience.   You may need to reshuffle present or future work assignments to help the employee get exposure to new skills and experiences.

Celebrate Growth

You are the manager. You have been involved in a personal dance of disclosure of intimate goals and ambitions, and perhaps even gained the trust of the employee enough to be invited to identify weaknesses and how to plug them.   As progress is noticed, you must provide recognition, and celebrate growth.   You are providing value and support, and coaching.   Your employee is providing their effort at self improvement.   Revel in the beauty of this win/win relationship that will be remembered years to come.   Celebrate success, one step at a time.   Maintain your support, provide encouragement.   If your self confidence allows, think hard of what are your own failings and their strength, and ask them in return to coach you on them.   Make it a reaffirming, humane partnership.

Enjoy your job.   You get paid to watch people grow and marvel at their own magnificence under your watch.   It doesn't get much better than this.

Work at the Next Level

For yourself as well as those you manage or mentor, I offer the advice that the best way to ensure you're ready for the next promotion, is to operate at that level long before the title.   If you act at the next level, your manager will be embarrassed into promoting you, or at a minimum will have an easy business case to pull it off.   Your peers will welcome your promotion as an example of a fair and just workplace, and that is wonderful too – you want their support.   It also helps you see whether you can handle the next level without sacrificing the things you hold dear, such as for e.g. work life balance.   It also helps you learn to become productive so that at the new level, your upcoming evaluations are not stinkers.

When you get good at working at the next level you will find that your current job gets easier, for as long as you end up doing it.   It's a very attractive proposition, and I hope you try it out.

Working to Rule

I believe very strongly that people will surprise you and themselves with what they can accomplish, given enough self confidence and your support.

I have mentioned in the introduction that the biggest gold we leave on the table is the unachieved results from the untapped talent of our employees.

Given the above, it follows that by and large, any goal setting on behalf of management will likely be translated into underachievement by the employees receiving said goal directives. If you tell a student that a "B" average is enough to graduate, that is what will be obtained at a minimum. If an "A" average is required for applying to a scholarship, then the scholarship hungry student will focus on that instead.

The individual goal setting documented in many companies at the beginning of the fiscal or marketing year, is actually a minimum bar over which an employee may be legally fired if it is not achieved. It shouldn't impress or wow the majority of your high performance team, or you for that matter.

I am fascinated by the ordinary application of the individual goal setting (contract) principle during organized protests by public transit employees. They can't strike legally, so the buses must run. How do they express their displeasure then? They "work to rule". They basically work to the goals of their contract, and no more. A one hour bus trip may now become a 2.5 hour adventure, with you surrounded by very angry fellow patrons, kids stranded elsewhere in the city, evenings commitments scratched, possible fighting between patrons and bus drivers. And while service anarchy seems to rule, the bus drivers are fulfilling the terms of their contract by law. Wow!

There is a large gap between minimum requirements, and professional performance. You will fail miserably as a manager if your people do anything resembling working to rule. You won't respect them, the environment, and yourself. Get away from that minimum bar, in the name of everyone's self respect. We need you to, as a leader in our society. Deadwood is not hired, it is created. By managers who allow de-motivation, sarcasm and cynicism to take over a group of employees. Squash it early and hard. Keep focused on new and wonderful achievements. Build a sense of pride and purpose. Remember the ones who breathe the biggest sigh of relief when work to rule ends, are the bus drivers. They have pride too. They had to pretend for a short while that they were insensitive, incompetent and jerks, to prove the point that what they did had value and was needed. It was killing them.

The Problem Employee

I see four main groupings for "problem" employees, depending on whether they are this way due to

- Death, Long Term Illnesses
- Divorce, Troubled Children
- Skills or Experience issues
- Bad Attitude or Emotional Immaturity

You cannot treat everyone the same way.

Death, Long Term Illnesses

Deaths in the family are a serious matter. The employee will understandably be shocked and depressed. A week off for bereavement leave, with pay, would be a proper show of support for them. Taking work off their plate for the next short while is a consideration, though the employee has to agree. Some of them welcome immersing themselves in their work in order to deal with the pain of the personal loss. Ask them what they need from you. Get ready to deal with this issue. It is unavoidable.

Long term illnesses are the worst thing to deal with. The employee suffers with no end in sight as they, aging parents or spouse fight battles with Cancer, AIDS, or other. It is a nightmare. Take pity; be considerate, resourceful in your support. It will one day happen to you, or someone you love. The employee is not in that personal hell by choice. Remember that employees are people first. Enlist the help of your team in redefining the job for the affected employee, providing a more suitable structure in terms of tasks and the time to perform them. If you can't find it in your heart to think this way, consider that an employee who was supported at such a difficult time, is likely to be a grateful and model employee later on.

While diverging off topic, my role model for how an Executive should act during troubled times is TJ Watson Sr., the founder of IBM. He kept people employed during the Great Depression, making machines that were perhaps not going to be sold. But when the economy turned around, he was ready to compete with a labor force that was skilled and fiercely loyal to him personally. They sang songs in his name at meetings! Would you sing a song to honor your current CEO? The IBM brand is today among the world's most valuable. Would you like to build an empire too? Look after your people.

Divorce, Troubled Children

This is a bit more complicated, because there is no obvious medical "treatment", or the employee may not come forth and disclose his problem. Even if you see it, they may not even admit it. They could be in denial. If it's a divorce, for example, it may take six months or three years from the day you find out, until it is resolved. You will have during and after, an employee who is at times angry or depressed. Keep in mind that in western society, more than half of the marriages end in divorce. Count on coming across this quite frequently as a manager.

Your employee could also have teenage children on drugs, or in trouble with the law; physically ill, suffering from mental health issues or any number of other things.

Be supportive, but understand your professional competence limits. You may be genuinely interested in their success, but you are not a psychiatrist. So refer them to the confidential Employee Assistance Programs, or Confidential Help Lines that are available through most employers. You can also suggest they can get a referral from a family doctor to see a counselor. The sooner, the better – but you can't force it. All you can do as a manager is remind them of their results, how you notice they are down, and suggest help for them so they get back to their normal selves and enjoy life more, the sooner, the better.

Skills or Experience Issues

Skills can be taught; experience requires time. If someone tries their best but can't handle the requirements of the job, they may need extra training from a peer, night courses at a local College or University, association with a mentor, your ongoing coaching, etc.

If the problem persists, maybe it is time to have a discussion on the benefits of doing a job they are good at, vs. the one they are not good at, and how do we go about helping them discover what other jobs are out there and how to help them move, before you are forced to fire them (don't make that last connection unless it is trending to that – the job fit conversation is much more constructive and preferred as a starting point).

Bad Attitude or Emotional Immaturity

I don't think that people have the right to show bad attitude in the workplace. They are in that job by personal choice (they applied at some point). Their bad attitude is damaging to others. That is not to say they ought to like or accept all they encounter by way of environment or company policy - far from it. But there is a professional way to show your displeasure, and bad attitude isn't one of them. That is barely acceptable in young children, and in teenagers under the understanding that they have not yet learned to control their hormones.

I would also like to say they don't have the right to show emotional immaturity, but I have come to accept that emotional immaturity is not within their control. If it took someone 37 years to learn to act like an emotional 8 year old, there aren't enough years left in my life to wait until they progress to emotional adulthood. Nor am I interested in watching it happen in my team. I need to move such people out, or if I can't, get out of their way. I suggest you read books covering Emotional Intelligence, and EQ, so you learn to recognize this if you don't already know.

Bad attitude is within the employee's control, in my mind – they are showing it on purpose. And there is no good that comes of it.

The way to deal with these destructive and insidious members of your team is to set and enforce clear boundaries. What is and is not allowed? You will call them on it at each and every transgression – and document it towards building a case for dismissal if it comes to that. You will also remove privileges as required: working from home will no longer be allowed, company cars should be taken away. They should be passed over for choice work. Policies on hours requiring their presence on the workplace will be enforced to the letter. Status reporting will be more frequent, and more detailed. You will have zero tolerance for late work or communication. Work assignments will be handed out with a preference for items that are easier to measure and leave less room for interpretation (so they don't invite debate when you evaluate the results).

You will also suggest anger management courses, time management and stress management courses, and that they enlist the services of professional counselors or psychiatrists.

You will at some point enlist peer pressure, making it known what you deem to be professional behavior and publicly praising it, or sending emails on company policy on the matter if such is available. The team will catch on, and in the short term it may be unpleasant and divisive – but the isolated individual will then have to choose between bending and moving on. The health of the team will always come first, in the end. You will also have to remove items of responsibility that require this individual to lead others.

You must keep your composure, no matter how much you are baited or the damage the employee is visibly causing. Don't react to unprofessional behavior with more unprofessional behavior. Your communication must be consistent and repetitive. The messages complement and reaffirm each other, over time. You don't hand out raises, awards, or bonuses beyond the bare minimum required by company policy – and you ought to consider requesting exceptions to this policy so you hand out nothing positive at all. Otherwise you would be sending the employee a mixed message. You don't improve the tone of the evaluation just because it may lower the abuse the employee will try to subject you to. You also won't get caught up in public debate. The department is not the public forum for you two to play the role of the dysfunctional couple.

Think positively: imagine how much better you will be as an interviewer, after suffering a few months with an employee like that? That is why I don't do sales jobs in interviews. I never try to convince someone that my company or my job opening is so wonderful. I go out of my way to describe what is good, and what is bad about the job. If you accept the job as described, you and I won't have problems with it in the future.

I will rather go on with an unfilled position, than accept an unscreened transfer from within my company. Because before I try to convince you to join my team, or accept you because you are "free", I need you to convince me that I would want to work with you. It's my high performance team at stake, and I won't let anyone mess with it.

Window Dressing

I have on occasions come across examples of window dressing. By this I mean a manager's efforts to make a troubling, high maintenance employee look better than they deserve, so they're attractive to another manager and thus more easily sent elsewhere.

You may have seen it too. Someone who you think does less than average work, is absent more than normal, can't be relied on for much, all of a sudden receives an award, and you guess by their speech, a good rating. A few months later, they move to another department, and your manager walks around looking about 10 years younger.

A few months after the transfer, you find out through the grapevine that the new team is making inquiries as to what your former peer was up to; she seems to be quite terrible in her new job. Would your team take her back? Your team declines.

That is window dressing. Making someone look better, feel better, to send them out of the team because it's easier than working on their flaws or firing them outright. The next team is stuck with a problem employee, and the clock to get her fired, given the job change and lack of history, got reset for another two years. Two years later, the dejected new manager looks happy in the hallway again, the employee took her growing list of awards into another job (with such awards and a growing portfolio of experience, she may even be promoted to management – oh the irony).

Please, if you have any respect for management as a profession and self respect as a leader, don't window dress! Do your homework, find out what is allowed by the law, your union contract, your HR policies, whatever else may be available, and work to cut off the gangrenous arm! You don't want to have someone pass you damaged goods, so don't do it to others!

Window dressing illustrates the requirement upon you to interview to the best of your abilities any internal transfers into your team. Unlike external transfers that may be eliminated through a relatively quick and painless flunking of probationary periods, full time damaged goods that are versed in company policy and union contracts will drive you to despair. Protect your team, the team's culture and yourself from window dressing.

Starting Out New Employees

I have personally observed that the first few weeks on the job have a tremendous impact on the new employee's adjustment to the new climate, and your ability to instill on them respect for the job now and into the future.

Keep them busy, very busy, from the moment they join your team. Do not allow them free time – they should socialize and meet new people as part of having to learn and achieve tasks you assign.

If they think the job is easy they will disrespect you, their peers, and themselves. This will manifest itself in poor attendance, requests for more money, lack of motivation, ongoing general complaints, and may lead to them leaving the company as soon as it serves the resume.

If you keep them extremely busy up front, they are constantly learning and achieving. That is why you hired them in the first place. They also remind their more seasoned peers that the job is good, and has potential and worth. It revitalizes the rest of the team, and allows you to deliver performance messages to individuals who need a correction. Eventually employees who were trending to become deadwood, have to decide whether to give up on turning the newcomer into a disgruntled underachiever, or maybe they need to leave the team for greener pastures elsewhere.

New employees don't know what happened earlier, nor why. They don't understand or acknowledge limits, since things must be doable if they can be assigned. When you set expectations, they will agree and buy-in as a matter of course. They are your single greatest lever to the transformation of the culture within your organization. Because they're new, keen, energetic and don't know better. And for a very short time, they're trying to impress by attempting to deliver on the impossible. Don't waste this opportunity.

It is all too common that employees join a firm to an empty desk, no computer yet available, no phone, no passwords, no training, no mentor, no buddy, no work assignment. When I got my first full time job, I found I actually didn't have a job! My manager didn't need me! So when I recovered from the shock, I asked for permission to go find who could use my services in trade for my training. He liked that. I got my first award 12 weeks into the job, and within 6 months I had learned every task that department had to offer, working 50% overtime. I had helped everyone without exception achieve their work commitments. I was also unconsciously networked. But if my reaction had been an equally valid "this is what I went to school for? This is why I turned down offers with your competition?" I am pretty sure things would have gone differently. Don't gamble the employee will take their career in their own hands right from day one, to compensate for your mismanagement. Many will quit within a few years, and badmouth your company to whoever cares to listen. And you will have lost good talent to the competition.

Interviewing People

The single greatest contribution of a manager to his or her team is in the selection of candidates to join it from the outside. Picking winners or losers will fundamentally affect the team, the culture, what can be achieved, and how you spend time as a manager dealing with these people in the future.

What do you interview for? Obviously you need to scan resumes for a minimum of skills and experience, though skills can be taught and experience gathered through time – most importantly you are looking for maturity, achievement, flexibility, character, and ability to learn and work in teams, communication skills.

You are also making notes in the interview – will this person fit into your future vision for this team? Is this person going to lower my headaches?

I believe that the last thing a manager needs to do in an interview, what is to be avoided like the plague, is a sales job. I explain to candidates what the job entails, and this is followed usually with my view of the pros and cons of the job, with the caveat that the distinction is based on my value system. Then I ask the candidate to keep this in mind based on his value system, because the only successful outcome of the interview is a proper fit between the candidate and the job environment at hand. A bad fit will cause trouble for all. No sales jobs from me. I explain further that while I expect people to overplay their goodness in a resume, beware of lying – it will hurt the job fit if caught after the fact, with dire consequences and time wasted for us all as I will have to fire them. Normally by then I have the candidate's undivided attention, and we can focus on the common problem of determining a job fit. Win/win.

To illustrate, I once hired an outstanding technical writer. He came to see me weeks later to vent about some truly unpleasant aspects of the job. I listened attentively, for I agreed with him anyway. I then asked if he was done, and he said yes. My next question I believe was "So?" He thought for a bit and then started laughing. "Oh no, you told me it would be like this at the interview". He burst into more laughter and left my office. I didn't hear those complaints again. He was more than welcome to improve the place as he saw fit. I didn't trick him during the interview; he chose to join the team knowing the warts beforehand. It was his decision, and I was going to make him own it.

I like throwing people off balance during interviews, to see how they react under stress. I am not evil, truly. But if you want to know someone, observe them under stress. Under nice conditions, we can all be civilized. The veneer of civilization peels off when the heat is on. And what will test the person's ability to fit and contribute will be his or her ability to deal with the task at hand, under stress.

I like testing people's resourcefulness, especially considering that after years trying to look for the way to achieve the answer at the back of a university textbook, they now need to tackle open ended problems with poorly defined situations and parameters, working with and for people who are unpredictable sometimes, and not always agreeable. All the while they are finding their own limits. So I give out lots of puzzles, and expect them to explain why certain paths were chosen for the solution. You would be amazed how many University graduates can't grasp basic grade school arithmetic. Or cannot communicate what is in their heads under stress. Refuse to hear tips and hints. Go back to broken solutions just because they can. Will argue with you the fairness of the test (life is fair?), when it was actually a test of their character.

There is no job more important than your screening of interview candidates. Get good at it, through endless practice.

Don't hire the first person who seems to be adequate. You either want this person on the team, or you should pass. You must be strengthening your team with every new hire. It is very expensive to hire and train people, and your team is counting on you to deliver the very best for the money. Demand excellence.

In the end, here is the acid test: you will hire someone because they will lower your risk; they will make your headaches go away, by taking them upon themselves. That is why you are interviewing them, right? If you don't feel your stress level decreasing from visualizing that person on the job, move to the next candidate. Trust your instinct.

Puzzles

Here are some of the puzzles and what I was after, when I gave them to people during interviews:

1/ Replace the letters below with numbers from 0 to 9. If you for e.g. pick E = 7, all E's will be 7, and no other letter can use it.

```
        SEND
+       MORE
==========
       MONEY
```

You would be amazed as to how many University graduates will take time and require your help to figure out that M from the Totals line can only be 0,1, which is key to solving this puzzle. After all, what numbers could constitute a valid "carry into the next column" in an addition?

2/ There are 4 people in a cave, and it's dark. They have only one lamp. They must use the lamp to travel to shelter nearby. The people can travel alone or in groups of two, but the lamp must always travel with them. They do the trip one way, at different speeds. So the time taken by "A" to do the one way trip is 1 minute. "B" is 2, "C" is 4, "D" takes 5. When two people travel together, naturally the trip takes as long as the slowest person. Find the fastest time to move everyone over.

If "A" carries everyone over, the trips cost AB + A (has to return with the lamp) + AC + A + AD = 13 minutes. But this is not the fastest. Find the fastest.

3/ Bridges of Konigsberg: You can look this up on the internet, but the point of this famous problem is to see when the interviewee will realize that it can't be solved. I think it's important to find a problem with no solution, even better if you make it a scenario where there is an impossible tradeoff of work pressures (such as how to choose between shipping a product with known problems on time, or shipping it late but working as desired – I really like how people squirm on this one). See how they come up with an answer, and how they defend it. You are hiring character, after all.

4/ Chess Puzzle: I devised this original chess puzzle for interviewing purposes. White has King on h8, Pawn on h7, Knight on a1; Black has King on e7, and it's Black to move and draw. Provide a hint: the next move is either Kf7 or Kf8. When solved, move the knight to another position. When that is solved too, ask for the rule: how is the king move related to the initial placement of the knight?

This problem I gave to people who knew nothing of chess, even if it meant my having to explain the movement of the pieces first. Is that fair? I am interviewing people to hire them to solve problems that neither of us can foresee, so I would say it's very fair. Interestingly enough, the less the candidates knew about chess, the better they fared. They tackled it for what it was: a problem to be solved, under pressure.

5/ Monty's problem: This famous game show problem usually leaves people passionately arguing for the merits of their solution whether they're right or wrong. The internet has the problem as well as solutions and simulations to back the solutions.

You can have puzzles for creativity, awareness of tradeoffs, grace under pressure, honesty, whatever you value. Ensure you avail yourself of any and all legal means to increase your odds of determining whether the person you're interviewing is a good fit for your team. Don't go on resumes alone, or what they say in an interview. Even if you become a professional interviewer one day, don't assume you're not facing a professional interviewee.

Dress for Success

A monkey in a suit is still a monkey, surely – but a very nice looking monkey ☺

If you are trying to impress people into accepting you, you should see what affinity you may show towards them. If you are visiting a customer, how about modifying your dress code somewhat for a more comfortable fit with the customer's environment?

You can demonstrate individuality through the excellence of your individual results and contribution. If you don't want to be taken for a joke, don't look like one. Nobody dragged you out of bed this morning to come to work; you chose to go to work. The place existed before you and will likely exist after you. Use common sense. Watch your peers and your boss, and dress accordingly.

Diversity and Conformance

There is at times an uncomfortable and unstable gap between stated respect for diversity by the employer, and expectations to have diversity respected by the employee. Disparities in interpretation often times fall under the specter of what is and what is not "politically correct", and far too often this leads to abuse both in favor of as well as against the alleged minority or interest group for reasons that have precious little to do with the individual's contribution to the business. I am amazed at how many people think they have a right to impose their cultural, religious, societal views on the workplace, and it is not because I am not enlightened as to the value of diversity – Canada is my 3rd country, English my 3rd language, my marriage is interracial, to name a few of my personal attributes.   To make matters worse, companies at times fuel destructive societal conflict by selecting and rewarding individuals based on factors that are not completely and unequivocally based on merit.

I've witnessed and experienced discrimination based on background and accent (ignorant and insecure people fear and mistrust backgrounds they don't know, and it's hard not to have an accent when you know and frequently use several languages). I have no illusions that discrimination will go away in my lifetime, given the ignorance of the individuals who perpetuate it and the teaching they naturally must be providing their children.

But I believe that to be respected for who you are, you need to first respect everyone else. And if you join a group, their rights come first. That is the price of membership. By showing your worth, you may influence a change in the culture to better suit your needs, in due time. I believe that intelligent leaders understand that leaving anyone out of the picture, anyone marginalized for a non-business reason is a price that no successful business can afford.   So if you or your employees want to change the world in the name of Diversity, kindly think hard about how you'll go about doing it. It's not about quotas; it's about seeing problems in new ways, solving them with new skills. It's about value.

My Father taught me that *our rights end where someone else's begin*. I agree.

Management vs. Leadership

To me, **management is about the optimized use of resources to most efficiently and effectively get the job done. Leadership is about going where nobody has gone before, and when you look back people are following - and do so gladly - because of you**. I marry the two, to get the best of both worlds: when I am given an area to manage, I figure out how it could be run in the most effective and efficient manner possible. I also get the team to work out with me wonderful new ways we could generate value for whoever deserves it, while we evolve as professionals. The savings from the improved management are applied under high morale and productivity to the new leadership vision, generating new value and a new way to do business. This new business now requires management, and the team is also hungry for a new leadership vision of what else may be accomplished… and the cycle repeats. I love it.

Employees don't always respect the power inherent in the position of management. They may fear it, but that's not the same as respect. Yet people follow a leader because they want to, they willingly agree to be influenced by the leader. In other words, there is some power due to the title bestowed upon the manager from above, but the real power is bestowed upon the leader from below. The worker bees that get the job done, and they alone control quality, cost, and time. They control whether to exceed expectations, meet them, or work to rule. They choose whether they want to follow. The best processes in the world will fail in the hands of disgruntled employees. But motivated employees will overcome all manner of obstacles in support of a leader's vision.

In American baseball, often times I saw teams change coaches as a response to underachieving players. For years that puzzled me. If the players who are paid so much more than the coach refuse to perform as per their salaries, why change the coach? Answer: because it's easier to change the coach. Then sometime later a new coach shows up, of comparable worth to the departed one, and the team performs magic on the diamond. What happened? The players set up the previous coach? Power from below.

I was further amused by the merry go round of coaches during the period I was a fan of the National Hockey League. Coaches were fired, hired overnight by another team in the league, and then fired again, hired again... maybe the coaches were competent, and the teams were switching coaches until players were in the mood to play for them? It sounds outrageous to me, a complete violation of the tenets of professional obligation by the players who are obliged to perform for their lofty salaries out of respect for the fans. What a powerful example of Power from Below. Coaches came and went in a "coach/team job fit" dance as the League prayed feverishly for the legalization of human cloning, so it could put a charismatic leader such as Scotty Bowman behind every bench. You try more for some people. Are you intending to be one of those people? Is the word Charisma used to describe you? I know of no higher praise.

Risk vs. Responsibility: The Art of Delegation and Empowerment

All tasks worth doing carry some level of risk. The manager is always responsible. You delegate a risky task to a subordinate. Who gets the credit when it goes well? Who takes the bullet when it goes foul?

In my opinion, you delegate the task, not the responsibility. You will hand out the credit, and own the blame. If it looks unfair, it isn't. You are offloading work, and that is your benefit. Hope you did a good job setting expectations and training. You need to show you are a leader worth following, and they can't follow you when you are behind them.

If you explain this arrangement up front along with the assignment, the employee will value your trust and protect your vulnerability. Out of this, teams are built. If they screw up, they will watch to see if you keep you word – make sure that you do. Your only request should be for a debrief for what went wrong, and how was it preventable so we can learn to avoid this particular failure in the future. Thank the employee for their effort, and be genuine about it.

Then get ready to find out what kind of organization you work for, really. How you are treated as you take the bullet will teach you more about your own superiors than any other activity you might have taken on. Eventually if you're punished, the team will rally around you – a manager like you is a prized commodity, and your replacement would have likely hurt them. They won't let you down in the future if they can possibly help it. They will do their very best to ensure your success. Soon you and your team are the envy of the entire organization. Other managers, less insecure will go out of their way to say your team is unprofessional, has too much fun, is too happy and thusly must be slacking, etc. It is nearly unfathomable to a non charismatic manager who wields the power of her position like a cattle prod, how you could run a high morale, high performance team by maintaining a club like environment.

Eventually you will grow your folks enough so that you will see them empowered to try to do things without you telling them. Then you better strap on the seatbelt, the bus just became a racecar. You will likely have a hard time filling your workweek, at this point; the problems are disappearing faster than you can find them. Value grows everywhere. Productivity goes thru the roof, along with morale. You will fill your growing free time with more valuable activities like customer contact, and mentoring other managers. Your job just became fun. Enjoy it ☺

Project Management Fundamentals

The purpose of your team's existence is to produce something that is expected by your sponsor and stakeholders (usually customers), with limited resources. If you don't produce output in an efficient and effective manner, do things right and do the right thing, you will be eliminated.

The Iron Triangle

The Iron Triangle of project management has three sides: Content (what we do), Cost (resources it takes to produce what we do), Schedule (when does it need to be done by).

In your organization, one of the three will be an immovable variable, and the other two can be tinkered to make the project viable. For example, if your team is managing the next Presidential Election, you don't have the ability to miss your deadline. The Election Day is fixed.

Or if you work at a Hospital, you may find that Cost is the immovable constraint, because Funding is very much limited.

Or if you are programming the computer for the next space launch, or the software for a pacemaker, you will find that Content is the immovable constraint. A navigation computer that "misses" the targeted planet, or a pacemaker that misfires, are not acceptable output even if delivered on time and on budget.

The Critical Path

Once you understand the requirements of your organization, you will build a plan that has

- Work Breakdown Structure (WBS - complete and approved list of tasks and activities required to complete the project)
- Sizing of the items in the WBS
- Causality, precedence requirements or linkages between WBS items (what needs to happen before a particular task can start?)
- Assignment of resources to WBS items
- Identification of the Critical Path (this being the path, sequence of linked activities that leads to the completion of the project in shortest possible time). By definition, any delay along the Critical Path leads to a delay in the completion of the project.

Suggested Management of the Project

I find it best to manage the project by

- Exception: tell me what is NOT happening as planned, and I trust you to imply that everything else is fine.
- Critical path: tell me what is putting the final date at risk. Anything not on the critical path, I don't really need to get involved in.

Of course that is my personal style, and it does work very well for me. But you could feel pretty uncomfortable on budgetary items in your field, so you may want to add

- For non critical path items, tell me when an item starts eating into the contingency funds

Store the initial plan, and all approved change requests somewhere for public access and consumption, for reference. Store all proof of completion in the same place.

Lessons Learned

This is tricky stuff, but mandatory to ensure that your team learns and grows before the next project.

You must find a way to capture what went wrong, and why. Then spend the effort required to come up with root cause analysis (the beginning of the chain of events that led to failure), and the preventative plans and recommendations that prevent the identified undesirable events from reoccurring in the future. You must do this by focusing on the problem, not the person who made the mistake. Here is the mantra: *"I don't care what you did wrong so long as you learn from it. Better yet, teach us all so we learn from it too"*. Thank all contributors from the bottom of your heart and with the deepest gratitude your can muster on behalf of the entire management chain you represent, as well as their peers and our customers, for speaking up for the betterment of us all.

90% Perception

For better or for worse, your job as a manager is judged mostly on what people perceive you think and do.   Don't count on anyone asking if they're not sure, they'll invent a likely answer and accept it as truth.   Asking you what you meant, may put them at personal risk.   Assuming they understand what you meant, does not.   Or so they think.

How you carry yourself, you confidence, assertiveness, your reaction to stress, input and news, are constantly being evaluated and you're catalogued accordingly.

The information vacuum you leave on the table, the unspoken obvious points, people will fill in for you, and you will end up owning it.   Nobody second guesses what they think you believe in, nobody will ask you to confirm.   What you do and say, and how you say it, will be the embodiment of your value system.   What you meant to say?   Irrelevant. You were in a bad mood because your furnace didn't work the night before and you froze overnight?   They'll never know.   They will probably think your short fuse is related to a mistake recently made, and you're barely controlling your anger over it.

It is remarkable how quickly you lose your true self and become an image, when you become a manager.   How unapproachable you become, so people will assume things about you in ignorance that you may find abhorrent.   Get over it.   Own your image, try to have it match your beliefs, and get ready to roll with the waves.

This is a tough lesson for you to impart to your team leaders, but the sooner you figure it out, the sooner you can teach it.   Because out of such team leaders you may find the manager to replace you, and there's no time to start learning the Perception rules like the present.   Learn to manage your perception.

Learning from the Masters: Advertising in the Car Industry

Those of us who acknowledge the value of perception intellectually, but haven't been able to make the disciplined mental leap required to proactively manage the perception we exude professionally, need only to look at the masters of the craft in our economy: the car industry.

The car industry spends lots of money on advertising.   Let's look at a repeating theme in their ads:

You see a car accelerating to phenomenal speeds, then driving at these speeds in the rain, on ice, on mountain turns; the driver is happy, well dressed, has beside him or her a fine specimen of the opposite sex, though on occasion said specimen is waiting for them at the destination. Pedestrians and other drivers can't help but turn their heads at the passing of your fine vehicle.   It's about Freedom.   Power.   Sex Appeal. Image!

Now I don't know where you live and drive, but where I live and drive, things are a little different. The speed limits are typically forcing me to drive at about ¼ of what my speedometer says my car can achieve, and the police are more than willing to enforce this limit in all manner of creative and typically sneaky ways. If the police don't slow me down, traffic or construction will, anyway. More often than not, I have to share the roads with drivers who make driving alongside them, a hazardous proposition. I have seen people drink, eat, put on makeup, gesticulate with their driving hand while the other hand was on the cell phone, and even read while at the wheel. The roads where I drive have potholes. Drivers typically slow down on my side of the road to get a look at drivers getting tickets, or motorists changing tires, or car accidents on the other side. The car commercial must be describing life in another planet. But that description sells an image, and that image sells the car.

More fascinating still, and proving the true genius of the people who handle the advertising side of the car industry, is the relatively recent migration from "Used Cars" to "Pre-owned Vehicles". I can't recall when exactly this happened, but I remember a time when cars would be classified as "new" or "used". Now they are "new" or "pre-owned". What's in a label? Perception is everything. Try to feel the difference by walking through these attributes:

Used Car	Pre-Owned Vehicle
Worn	Gently used
Tired	Running
Limping	Able
Cheap	Value
Needs Work	Almost New
Rusted	Well Maintained
Deal	Keeps Value
Buyer Beware	Warranty
How many owners?	Owners care
How broken is it?	Previously loved
Am I being cheated?	Vehicles outlast owners

Shocking, isn't it? Words are important. Images around those words affect your willingness to buy, and for how much. Were I buying a car, I'd label it "used" to drive down the price. Were I selling it, I'd label it "pre-owned" to get a higher price.

Think of the mental gymnastics and associated changes in acceptance, attributes, predispositions, and preconceptions generated by the image the words convey. Manage your image. Manage your perception.

The Power of Leverage

To be a successful manager's manager, you must work through the managers who work for you. They are the lever for your productivity. If you improve yourself personally by 10%, a tremendous accomplishment, that is ok for the company. Since your overtime is likely unpaid, it's not too big a deal but well done, anyway. Keep up the good work. Now let's assume that every manager has 10 people reporting to him or her.

If you improve the ten managers working for you by only 5%, you would now see a full half-manager improvement in the team of 10 managers (5% x 10). That is 50% of a person, clearly much better than your previously wonderful 10% personal growth.

If you cause the improvement of a mere 2% for each of the people reporting to your managers (10 x 10 = 100 people in total), a trivial achievement, you would see a full two extra persons added to your organizational capability (2% x 100 = 2). That is the power of leverage. Smaller gains leveraged further are not only more easily achievable, but also most desirable.

I look at how to improve everyone in my organization, a minimum of 5% per annum. It translates to a paltry 2 hours per week. Presently I manage about 180 people in three countries. That adds up to 9 people, or roughly a new department, every year. Pretty good uh?

From Team Leader to Manager

Managing a team after you have demonstrated you were a marvelous team leader is tricky, you need to keep an eye out for things you may be used to doing that perhaps are no longer welcomed in your new role:

- Being on top of everything (because to do so, you would micromanage your team leads into hating you, or curtail their productivity at a minimum; plus your scope of responsibilities just grew too much, you don't have the cycles to be so curious)
- Working on everything with burnout always a risk (need to learn delegation and leverage)
- High volume communication (aim for less energy and more finesse)

In addition, you need to make doubly sure that you are not displaying favoritism towards anyone who was your bosom friend up to the day before your promotion to management; conversely you need to show that you're not prepared to go on a witch-hunt to the detriment of anyone who you didn't see eye-to-eye with prior to your role change. Your fairness, impartiality, and open mindedness will be observed, commented on, and judged.

Becoming Manager of Managers

Your approach becomes less hands-on, or at least from a visible point of view. You now need to work on coaching in private, the managers who report to you. They have to be seen as the leaders of their teams. If you can't resist the temptation to take visible charge of everything, you will in effect be emasculating, disempowering your managers. They will become mostly secretarial extensions of your persona, if not frustrated outright into leaving your team. You won't be able to get them to grow, because you yourself will be blocking their growth.

Your ego may suffer in that other than visibly setting high level direction and having individual meetings with your managers' people, you won't be seen much if you do your job well. You may wonder how to defend and justify your value. Once you gain adequate amounts of self confidence, and you have done good work growing the strength of your managers, you will be freed up for new high value add roles such as customer relations, setting future strategy, for example.

You need to take a proactive hand at setting strategic goals for the area, and communicating them so that the entire organization is lined up towards an effective and efficient alignment in their support. You must provide the vision that is broader than any individual department's concern, and every department must find a way to line up with it. Keep in mind that while you may have initiatives key to your area that change every few months, or yearly depending on the tactical needs of the overall area, the strategy must be solid enough to withstand short term hiccups.

As the manager of managers, you are also providing budgetary guidance to your managers, not just for projects but also salary planning, bonuses, awards, retention vehicles (stock options, perks), among others. You are the consistency check so that some teams don't feel they're unfairly represented under your system, compared to their peers. Whether you assign budgets at the department level or get every manager into a room to agree on how to use it up to the last penny, you are the final check and balance for fairness. Most importantly, you are the creator of an environment of trust where all the managers working for you are able to feel they can channel their energy to their job at hand without worrying about how you treat them compared to their peers. You and your managers are far too busy with your jobs, to be able to afford to divert precious energy towards wondering what Machiavellian machining is going on in your organization.

The Walls between Management and Employees

Oftentimes, the point of such a distance is to allow the manager to deliver tough messages that would have otherwise been impossible at a peer level, such as:

- Sorry, I decided to skip your salary increase this year
- Your results are trending down, you need to stop the slide
- You won't be getting promoted
- I gave the project you wanted to someone else
- You're fired
- You need to move to another team, they need you more
- I need to give your team leading job to someone else

But do you really need to be aloof and in another world to be comfortable delivering such a message? I try to not have walls, myself. In a high performance team, my job as the team's manager is just another role. I do my job when I evaluate my friends. The results require a numerical reading, and I am the thermometer. Kindly respect the difficulty of my position, I want to go back to a good relationship the moment immediately following my tough message to you, and I want to see how I can help you get better.

I believe that if you respect the individual, you can deliver any message you want, and you will have their permission to do so. In some cases, they will feel bad they made you do your job as you did. Employees are that good, oftentimes.

So if you need the wall, the distance, go ahead. If you don't, that is ok too. Both ways, you have a role, and your role requires mutual respect and precise communication. If you have done your job and have set expectations and provided feedback throughout, no ugly message is undeliverable. Better yet, ask them to help you never deliver such a message. Employees, like you, are very fair and responsible if they value the relationship at hand.

In my experience, the vast majority of employees will accept pretty much any message from you, however unpleasant, if you as their manager are deemed to be a consistent and fair messenger and evaluator. Whatever you do or say, ensure you're fair in thought and deed.

Must Have, Should Have, Nice to Have

In every relationship, there needs to be an agreement as to the core values to be respected. Those would be the Must Have needs and wants. These are non negotiable, define you, and you or your employees will walk if the relationship does not honor them. We must have food and shelter. The work environment must be devoid of sexual harassment.

The Should Have needs and wants is a larger area that encompasses the potential for rich negotiation. They are not deal breakers, but they really enrich your life and that of your people. We should have raises that keep up with the increases in cost of living, but we won't die if they don't.

Nice to Have items are the stuff we normally don't demand, and nothing untoward will happen to the known Universe if they never come through. But when they do, they repay with tremendous payoffs any investment therein. It would be really nice if every now and then, our manager would celebrate our birthday with a coffee, or give us a thank you note for a job well done. Sure we already got paid for our labors, and what's a coffee worth anyway - but we'd go far for someone who displayed such small gestures.

The Must Have items get someone physically present in the workplace. To your company's Finance department, these "buy" a body to warm up a chair. The Nice to Have items get them working at their highest levels of creativity and productivity. It's the little things that validate our humanity. The Nice to Haves feel really good.

To you and the project managers, the levels of productivity, results, customer satisfaction and what may be accomplished by employees well looked after in the Nice to Haves, is the pot of gold at the end of the rainbow. Never mind that working in such an environment is simply wonderful.

Networking

What is networking, and why should you care?

It's useful to imagine the organization you belong to, as a spider web. Information flows along the web, between any two points, in any number of ways. Pretend that at any intersection, there is someone who can inform you of the information that passed through there. If they inform you, they're part of your network. If they don't, they aren't.

It's pretty easy then to visualize that the greater the numbers of people at the intersections who are willing to tell you about some piece of information, the more up to date you will be. Conversely, the smaller the number of intersections with your best interest in mind, the more in the dark you will remain.

That is the information network. Important also is the decision network. If the number of decision makers on your side increases, the better your odds of gaining acceptance to your ideas or needs. If your network is small, the greater your efforts to convince a number of people who don't know you or trust you, of the merit of your ways. Even more concerning, you may not even be aware that a decision was in the making.

So we can define your network from the perspective of your job as manager, as the number and spread of people gathering data and supporting your needs across the wider organization. The wider the network, they better off you are.

Networking carries positive and negative connotations. The negative ones conjure images of people showing a deep fascination with the mundane interests of their superiors, merely because they believe that by sucking up to these superiors, they will incur their favors. It's about "who you know", more than "how good you are" or "who you are", and some people will overlook moral and ethical boundaries to enter into such relationships. Alas, we all see examples of this in the workplace... yuck!

The positive aspects of networking can be summarized quite simply in your increased ability to do your job because you now have access to more relevant and correct, timely data to help with your decision making. Also you have the trust, access and ear of the decision makers. Value is being provided to and from everyone in your network. This kind of networking is vital to your job.

Yes, you can network to attain remuneration and favors far exceeding your merits. Whether you practice that kind of networking, I leave to your value system and work ethic – and always keep in mind the admonitions of safe sex, the fair retributions of karma, and the punishments due you from a just God if you abused your power along the way. To the rest of us, I encourage you to network as a mechanism to let you and the decision makers get to know each other better, so that you and they may be more effective and efficient at the job.

Experience and Age Discrimination

I find it difficult to comprehend how come our society has learned to discard so much knowledge and experience as is embodied in some of our older employees. True, in some highly technical and dynamic fields where technology is advancing faster than the time required for someone to attain an advanced degree on a particular topic, it makes sense to concern oneself with the hiring of some so called current skills to complement the experience in your team. And perhaps the cosmetics industry would collapse if people would realize that laugh lines are so beautiful, and that the beauty of a woman is in the twinkle in her eye and a passionate face that holds mystery and promise irrespective of age, rather than silicone and cosmetic surgery… but I digress.

One would think that the employees who have been with us the longest, who have experienced, perhaps thrived through periods of considerable societal and economic turmoil, who have seen the consequences of poorly run projects and decisions and know how to improve upon them, would be worth their weight in gold as in-house consultants. But that's not always the case, again, because we're still trapped by what we can measure. We don't have a measurement for the value of experience. What we can measure, may indict them.

Often times said employees feel they have to apologize for a greater entitlement of vacation days, perhaps higher salaries, and the unwillingness to work long overtime or fly across the world on a moment's notice due to health or family commitments. Yet these employees can save society millions by counseling leaders and managers on upcoming decisions, preferring to prevent a crisis rather than look the hero while fixing it. Yes you value the energy of new and skilled talent attempting the impossible, but you also need the value that experience and confidence earned during tough times bring to the job.

When I first started to work full time upon graduation from my engineering degree, I made a point to befriend the two most seasoned gentlemen in my area. One a former manager, the other a former repairman, they feared nothing and nobody. With a fabulous sense of perspective and a delightful sense of humor, they generously gave me all the wisdom I could handle and then some. What I learned from these people, professionally and personally, serves me to this day.

My friends retired after long and honorable service, and I still miss them. I hope they know wherever they are, how valuable their counsel still is to me.

Do your best to fight age discrimination at your company. It can't afford the loss of experience. And until people naturally retire or move on to other work, do your best to listen for any experience they care to share.

The Shotgun and the Scope

You can help yourself get stronger, as well as your team, if you keep this observation in mind that I was able to gleam by watching truly exceptional people. I call my parable: The Shotgun and The Scope.

What separates the more junior employees, skilled to be sure and tremendously energetic but evidently inexperienced, from the very senior and seasoned Executive is how they would go hunting rabbits in a field.

The junior hunter would select a shotgun. Would carry a veritable wagon of ammunition, and shoot in all directions in the field in the hope of murdering the bunny who couldn't possibly escape such a rain of metal. The hunter would provide status on how good he was at reloading, how many shots he got off in a minute, the near complete coverage of the field, and the certainty that the bunny was successfully delivered as expected, we just need to find the body parts – there is a dog sniffing the trail of blood already.

The senior hunter gets herself a rifle, with one bullet and a huge scope. Pulls up a chair in a suitable location, goes quiet and waits for the rabbit. Calmly spots the animal, targets with a scope that would serve to count the rabbit's tail hairs, and dinner is served. The kill shot is clean, so the pelt may be used. There is no extra metal littering the field.

I have observed that Executives are more patient, focused, shoot just once, and with an economy of energy generally get what they want. Junior employees are energetic, noisy, messy, and the end result may be not quite usable right off the bat. They are learning, of course. We all are. I am forever trying to increase the size of my scope, ever since I observed the distinction I just offered. I believe it will make your team stronger if you apply this to yourself, and educate your team along these lines.

No animals were harmed in the writing of this book. Honest.

Regular Mental Checkups

You go to your doctor on a regular basis to make sure you are ok. That means checking for your pulse, blood pressure, and some blood work. Step on the scale, agree that indeed, you could lose some weight and will get around it sometime soon, and you're done for another year. Why do you do this? You want to know whether you can rely on your body functioning at some minimal level of performance for the next few months. And I do mean minimal. You may have the cardiovascular endurance of a cadaver, you may not be able to do a single pushup, both of which intellectually tell you that you are not doing well, but if the medical results come back "within acceptable limits", then great. You can still have red wine with dinner and a sandwich before going off to bed. Of course, and now in all seriousness: the better your physical conditioning, higher your daily water consumption, more balanced your meals and better your sleep, the better your body will be able to help you cope with stress, and the better mood you will be when doing your job, and generally enjoying life. But since we all know that, and I don't want to nag, let's go to something new.

What about your minimal mental health? Let's get serious. Your job as a manager REQUIRES you to be mentally on top of your game, every minute you are doing anything that is work related. What you do is amplified, good or bad, remember? So if you casually mutter a profanity under your breath, that customer situation will go south. If you don't realize you said under your breath "what a liar" the next time another manager presents project status, you will have trouble. If you yawn during an interview, things may get uncomfortable. If you're making a decision on product content, business case for more funding, etc. you are required to be sharp. If you're writing an evaluation, or explaining to an employee why a vacation has to be postponed, you better be on top of your game. If you're not on top of your emotional intelligence, you will not provide the proper words and arguments to support your needs, nor will you be able to spot opportunities in the speech of others. You must stay on top of your mental faculties. It is NOT optional. Your job is quite unforgiving on that regard.

Realistically speaking, you won't be on top of your game, every day. Some decisions must be postponed to a day when you're in control of your emotional intelligence, you're excelling at stress and anger management, and you are ready to listen attentively. Not every day will be like this! You are human! That is what makes you so charismatic, unique and lovable, right? ☺

Unfortunately, we are also not objective. Since in a room of ten people, you will hear 7 tell you quite confidently that they are better than average, you can be excused in your position of leadership for believing that you can deal with anything and everything, 7/24. And maybe you can try, but truth is, you shouldn't.

You need something to tell you that you are mentally healthy, and thus safe for yourself and others that day, week, or month. What would you use to figure this out?

I use two methods.   First of all, I have empowered my best friend to tell me in real time, on the spot, when I am not acting fairly, reasonably, or to the standards she knows I want to live and breathe by.   She knows I rely on her even when I am not receptive to her feedback, so she assertively gets in my face to tell me that this is not one of my better days.   I have trained myself to listen to this feedback.   You can do the same – what you require is someone who sees you daily, knows you well, and cares for you enough to stand up to you when you're becoming dangerous to yourself and others.

My second method is chess. I am a competitive chess player, and this may not work for you, but here it is anyway.   Chess is a logical and creative game; after attaining a high level of competence, relative playing strength will be affected positively or negatively by mood and confidence.

The Elo rating system used to rank chess players suggests that for a 200 rating point difference, the higher ranked player is supposed to win three games, and draw one game out of four games played against the weaker player.   The rating system is so accurate an indicator, that I know with confidence my odds of winning, drawing or losing a game with another player, just by looking at the ratings.

I play online chess, making moves every day in 6-18 games.   The server tracks my performance on a graph.   The graph and my rating changes tell me how well my mind is doing, how healthy it is.   It tells me that I was at a mental high point in March 2006, suffered a drop of 180 Elo points by June 2006, then rebounding to a localized high on September 2006, a localized low on December 2006.   Steady climb since then, nearly caught up with my high point. Lesson learned from this? First of all, I would be relatively concerned about major decisions made in June 2006, professional or personal – I wasn't at my best.   I would be bullish about my later decisions, and those undertaken in March 2006 while the first draft of this book was penned.

You can't always be at your best physically or mentally, so don't beat yourself up about it.   But you should be aware of your current state, and consider your present capacity and abilities to deal with the demands of your job as you carry on. How you figure out your present mental capacity and emotional intelligence, I leave up to you.   But remember that they are not constant, and they do affect the quality of your work and of your interactions.   Practice being self aware.

Building a High Performance Team

You can spot a high performance team. Not just by what it achieves, which is wonderful, but how the members look to the trained eye. They are

- Confident
- Happy
- Purposeful
- Energetic
- Supportive
- Forgiving
- Stable
- Motivated
- Proud
- Resourceful
- Flexible
- Successful

The team itself has an identity, defined by one or more of the following: purpose, symbol, code of conduct. The members of the team are priceless as individuals to each other, and the team larger than the individual. It is a place people want to belong to.

I asked a coworker as soon as I became a Father, what he thought ought to be my contribution to my kids, my legacy, and the bulk of my teaching. He didn't hesitate: "teach them confidence in themselves". The point being that they can learn many things, and get good at some – but at some point I no longer will be a part of their lives, and what I missed out on teaching them they may suffer at. But if I teach them to believe in themselves they will learn to excel at whatever they have to, and pick themselves up and keep going when they fall along the way. It's basically teaching them how to learn, how to be resourceful, how to be resilient. It takes care of everything. I can't predict their future, or their future needs. But I can arm them with what they need to face that future without me. So, that is what I give my employees: my confidence in them. They love it, need it, and it works. Also I give them a confident, supportive manager. I make mistakes, but I am confident it will all work out in the end. This takes a lot of stress out of the job environment, and it is required for building a high performance team.

Happiness, linked to high morale, is a key ingredient leading to productivity and results. Unhappy workers do slow, sloppy work. They also drain my energy and shut down my creativity, while doing this to themselves and each other.

Purpose is what gives us meaning to our day. It is the lens that focuses our energies and thoughts.

The enthusiasm and energy of a determined child will carry out tasks exceeding the expectations of the parents. It is no different in employees. That well of energy and purpose inside us, the ultimate productivity frontier, is what drives companies crazy looking for trinkets and motivational speakers to rally the troops (feel free to book me for this sometime).

We all fail sometime. We all face scary situations, and we often need the boost. I'm told the Germans have a saying: "when you laugh, everyone laughs with you – when you cry, you cry alone". You define your work environment and your character, as well as those of your peers, not by how success is handled but rather how failure is handled. You value your friends not by how they help you spend the winnings of a lottery, or a hot night at the casino. You value them when they are there for you when you lose your job, a parent, or have bad news from a doctor. High performance teams are chalk full of supportive team members, supportive of each other without exception or hesitation regardless of role. I have a couple of friends I know would fly over to see me if I said I needed them with me, without reason. Do you? Who would you do that for? What can be achieved from such a relationship? Better yet, what can't be achieved from such a relationship?

Forgiveness is required in a high performance team. As the goals must be high, the risk is high and occasional failure inevitable. Tolerance for eventual failure is available for anyone, by everyone, because all team members know that person must have tried their best. But we'll try again, and soon we'll succeed and laugh at it.

High performance teams have emotionally stable people. These folks are full of trust, confidence, support ... They are professionals. They work to higher standards, because their group is special and they contribute to that reputation by word and deed. They are passionate in a positive way. It comes from a record of achievement, a culture of winning. You know what to expect when you approach them. Whatever the crisis, "things will work out". High performance teams don't panic – they get the job done.

These folks are self motivating. They are professional in the true sense of the word. They get the job done, and it is done well and with expertise even in days they may not be feeling like it. They don't need to be cheered on, though of course it helps. They feed on each other's company. They know they are good, their team is good. They don't need you to tell them. You can save the trinket money for more junior parts of your area.

They are proud. It is not a "better than thou" pride, though other teams may think it so. They are proud to belong to something different and special, and are happy with that, whatever your feelings on the matter. Sport teams, military detachments, all build on this pride to support a culture that expects and attains awe inspiring excellence.

High performance teams have symbols, cultures, traditions that stand the test of time. Those are bigger than the constituent members. People will embrace symbols, and do for them things that mere mortals would consider either impossible, or at least questionable.

It takes that little, and that much, to set you apart. What sets your team apart, what makes them special?

Once the team feels unique and special, so do its constituent members. Though whether the special members form a special team or the special team attracts special members, can be debated. What makes the individual feel special as a member of a special team?

I belong to the *"Famiglia Gandolfi"* team. I believe I embody the legacy of my family's ancestors and name. I am the direct descendant and next in line of the Gandolfi family tree that has been tracked since 1580 AD, though the historical materials go back to the VI century.   My ancestors include painters, cardinals, judges, military heroes, and such. I have a lithograph of an ancestor who earned posthumous medals in battle for the independence of Italy.   Another ancestor willed her fortune to endow an orphanage. There is a Church in Pietra de' Giorgi, Pavia that houses remains of my ancestors. The Pope's Summer residence is Castello Gandolfo, attributed to the Gandolphus family from Genova – this matches family history. There are Gandolfi's scattered all over the world, but I'm "next in line". I wasn't given the latitude to underachieve, nor do I want it. Of course the family has had its share of scoundrels and they're also well documented. I have to make up for them, too.

It may sound silly to you, I realize. My ancestors are dust in graves I will likely never visit, and my grandfathers were dead before I was born. My progeny thus far is a collection of lovely daughters, so the line will likely follow into the next generation through one of my brothers. Few care these days about crests, nobility, family trees. But they are symbols that rally those who do care for them to attain a level of excellence to standards that would otherwise not be considered. I'm not being judged on my success by my contemporaries, or even by me. I am getting ready to be judged by my descendants for up to 2, maybe 3 generations. Maybe through this book, I may make it to 4 ☺

I didn't sprout from a rock, nor do I live in a cave. Otherwise this book would have stayed in my head, along with all manner of life wisdom and experiences I have gathered over the years that will follow me to my grave.   The teams I work in also feel the same way. We are special, unique, talented and magnificent. There is nobody in the whole wide world like us, and there never will be. The larger organization is also special, unique, talented and magnificent… and so on. Because I like me, and what I do is a part of me, I am motivated to do it well. My peers feel the same way. Together, we aim for wondrous things – for us nothing is impossible. This leads to a positive feedback loop, pushing further and further away the limits of what can't be done, surrounding ourselves with positive people who achieve good results alongside us. For as long as time and circumstances allow.

These feelings run deep. People remember fondly the great teams, the great groups they belonged to, with a poignant sense of loss when they're no longer a part of them. These groups carry their identity with them. You know at that point that they gave of themselves. They worked to a higher level and delivered beyond expectations, they experienced and witnessed miracles, perhaps even became a part of them.

You have to believe in yourself. You have value. You are priceless. You must have confidence. All of this and more applies to you, and the team you manage. Is there anything you really cannot do? Is there anything you team really cannot do? I didn't think so.

It is fun to be paid to feel good, surrounded by people who you like, and like you.

Welcome to the world of high performance!

Now it's time to reflect:

- What value do you contribute to your team?
- What value does your team contribute to the area?
- What value does your product contribute to your customer?
- What makes you proud to belong to the team?
- What makes team members proud to belong to the team?
- What needs to be done for the team to be successful?
- What needs to be done for the customer to be delighted?
- What are you learning?
- What are members of your team learning?
- What is your team's purpose?
- What is expected of you? List all stakeholders, before you answer.
- What is expected of your team? List all stakeholders, before you answer.
- What is the most amazing, the hardest thing you could achieve with this team?
- What, realistically, stands in the way? Make sure it's not you!
- What do you intend to do about it?
- What are you afraid of?
- What if you were not afraid?
- What are your team members afraid of?
- What if they were not afraid?
- Define progress.
- Have you identified what your people are good at? How are you tapping into it?
- Who is teamed up with you to make up for your blind spots?
- Who do you trust?
- Would you hire yourself?
- Would you pay yourself what you earn, out of your own money?

That will do for a start. Good luck with it!

Managing in a Union Environment

Organized labor and the governments they have supported have helped provide many benefits to workers and their families for generations. The definition of the workweek, child labor laws, pensions, employment insurance, minimum wage, employment equity, minimum safety standards in the workplace are just a few of the salient contributions to the workplace and society that we take for granted these days, started not so long ago by the aforementioned.

That's the good news.

The bad news is that while learning to deal with fairly oppressive and inhumane governments, management and owners, unions wound up copying some of the bad habits they organized to critique in the first place. To protect against old age discrimination, they enforced layoffs based on tenure and thus hurt typically younger employees. To protect against manipulating management, they enshrined into labor contracts procedures and methods that make it nearly impossible to fire incompetent employees. This hurts and demoralizes the better employees, and allows for the creation of a work environment many employees are not proud of. While taking on the fat bureaucracies of business, they built their own bureaucracies and political layers.

In my opinion, unionized labor in western culture has over the last few decades earned a reputation for poor quality output, low performers who can't be removed from the workplace short of getting caught stealing on video, employees who feel a sense of entitlement to spiraling wages regardless of their performance or the health of the business they belong to, resistance to change regardless of pressures from technology and globalization that they are ironically counting on to drive down prices of the consumer goods they purchase for themselves and their families, and most disheartening, a militancy using professional picketers to strike for strike's sake, even when the wages and benefits lost in the strike period far outpace the gains made in the contract.

Some citizens have lowered their support for some unions because of growing intolerance to the inconvenience due to the strike actions, for e.g. traffic gridlock, days children miss from school, University students risking the loss of a year of study, etc.

Unions in the government sector also face a negative and jealous look due to the growing advantage of their defined benefit pensions, funded in part by tax dollars from many private sector employees who are themselves being forced into acceptance of mostly defined contribution pensions and consequently longer years in the workforce (assuming they survive age discrimination after they're laid off or fired). Public sector unions are seen as spoiling their workers and keeping them rewarded beyond normal competitive forces that are the norm for the rest of society, which wouldn't be a problem except that the rest of society is mandated to fund through their taxes, so many of these union benefits. Given it is generally accepted that the private sector is the key driver of the economy and its employees most vulnerable to offshoring, layoffs, etc., why should the public sector employees be further ahead in comfort and security?

Within the employee group itself, support for the union leadership isn't unanimous. Workers know that strikes make them unpopular with the population at large, since by and large most concessions people would sympathize with are already enshrined in law or in the previous contract. Workers also feel a sense of detachment from the results of their efforts, since the progress of tenure is not related to output, skill or performance. Peer pressure is also a strong factor to lower performance to a lowest common denominator, so that "management won't exploit us". People eventually lose pride in their job, their output, and confidence in their marketable skills. They can't even enjoy a reward from management, since after all they would be seen as fraternizing with the enemy. In the private sector they can't count on job security either, because companies can move shop to another country with less labor trouble; also the union itself would sometimes rather lay off 5% of its members before making a 5% wage concession (this is something I cannot grasp).

Management in a union shop may feel that they are powerless to drive performance, instill a culture that welcomes change, drives better output and competitiveness. Their jobs feel more like babysitting and policing, than leadership. Management in a union environment sees high walls between management and employees, much energy spent on toeing the line and not enough working on improving the product, or maximizing the customer experience as compared to the non union shop.

Unions still have two main tasks to provide the modern worker with, in my opinion. The first one is the protection of pension benefits for employees, seeing as how governments have been so open about their future inability or unwillingness to care for the elderly in an ever aging population demographic. Yes, the cost of pensions can now translate into a measurable component in some North American cars, and in some cases, makes them uncompetitive. I don't think the pension component is a bad thing – it ought to continue, and maybe even grow. What I think it's a bad thing is that the workers who know there's a measurable pension sticker component in the cars they make, don't take pains to ensure it's worth the extra cost and value to the consumer in terms of quality and ownership experience. Lexus executives aren't ridiculed for pricing their flagship products multiples higher than the most affordable products by Toyota. This is not because they can't compare numbers, and the consumers are duped – it is because the consumer perceives the flagship Lexus products provide a different ownership experience than a Corolla. You can price a product at whatever price you want, if you make sure it's worth it.

The second job of unions is to provide together with the government, more exit barriers and a cool down period to executives tempted to make short sighted and unwise knee jerk reactions regarding moving labor to lower cost centers elsewhere in the world, when the decision is not good for much more than a short term stock manipulation. Together with management, unions can provide the solution for the long term and healthy stay of a company. After all, unions have a golden lever: employee productivity. If the union environment allows and encourages employee productivity and customer satisfaction, then the competition stands no chance at all. No labor savings in under skilled, under paid and inexperienced labor markets can compensate for a productive and customer driven, experienced labor force even at a premium wage. The more sophisticated the consumer, the more educated and wealthy she is. The aging population is a relatively wealthy one, and demands a quality of life unimagined by our grandparents. They are prepared to pay for value, and they want their children and grandchildren employed where they live.

I believe a manager in a Union shop has several challenges:

- He must be versed in the Contract. In a way this is not much different from learning Company Policy in a non-union shop, but seeing as how the relationship with the Union will often times be adversarial, and arbitrators, mediators, and Legal may be involved much more often, the Contract must be studied.
- He must be aware of what HR and Legal are willing to do about specific scenarios, even if the manager's role is obvious as per the Contract. It does little good for a manager to follow the contract to dismiss an underperforming employee, if HR and Legal won't back him up.
- He must be aware of what support he's to expect from his superiors, in this conflict rich environment
- He must be aware of what is the procedure to document unacceptable behaviors so to be able to fire people efficiently and effectively if they're not meeting requirements. Union shops are fertile ground for abuse under the misinterpreted protection of Affirmative Action, so extra care is needed.
- He must be able to lower the management – employee barrier with the employees who truly want to make a difference.
- He must be able to find ways to reward effort and behavior worth emulating. Of course not phrasing it as "for supporting the company vision", since that's not the environment you work in, anyway. "For finding ways to improve our customer's experience" ought to be a valid motto whether you're curing leprosy pro bono, or building shopping malls. Whatever business you're in, whatever your environment, there are fundamentals to your business and they're recognized to be good regardless of management – labor relations. Keep your speech, motives, awards, actions tied to these, and you can manage anytime, anywhere, anyone.
- Try your best to maintain and present your humanity first, and then your role as manager. This may save you some grief when the day comes you're to cross the picket lines, manned by people who are expected to abuse you.
- Try your best to break the job down into activities towards a goal, separating them from who is doing them. If people agree on the job at hand, they know why it needs to be done and how, you depersonalize the assignment of required tasks. Your best protection against the inefficiencies and ineffectiveness of a high conflict and low trust labor – management environment, is a highly skilled and proud employee who knows what to do without being told.
- You must have empathy for the unionized employee, and try to minimize the conflict potential between you two. Since the biggest determinant of job

satisfaction is your manager, and in a union shop, the manager is the enemy, how much could a union employee actually enjoy their job? Imagine going to work every day, to report to the enemy? To increase their job satisfaction and their productivity, their pride in their work, you must take steps to lower conflict and defuse the adversarial relationship your boss and the union bosses, the contract have willingly or unwillingly created.

- Understand that many unions promote into their management people who excel at organizing and militancy, negotiation. These are not necessarily the top skills or experiences they require for the job of managing the union hierarchy towards the goal of strengthening the company and employee's positions to the long term benefit of all. The union hierarchy is normally unqualified to help grow the business at a partnership level with the professional managers running the company. It's a matter of training, and profession. No matter how brilliant the top general of a country's army, it takes a leap of faith and no small amount of denial to imagine they will be qualified to assume the role of competent president of the same country (I have lived under army rule, in Argentina).

- Finally, keep in mind that in spite of the environment, employees want the same as everywhere else. Recognition, compensation, stimulating work, pride, fairness, safety, are but an obvious subset of their reasonable needs. You want these things yourself, and for your children. You have a lot of common ground already. Try to build a partnership, and go for long term win/win. Good luck!

About the Author

I was born in Buenos Aires, Argentina, the oldest of five children. I lived there until my parents decided to emigrate to Canada because the military government of the day was kidnapping, torturing and killing people by the thousands. It colors your view on life and authority, when you are exposed to Martial Law before becoming a teenager. I have memories of waking to machine gun fire, of being taught what questions were not to be asked. I saw first hand the abuse of authority on a grand scale.

In Canada I was exposed to mind boggling political tolerance, un-watered down milk, newspaper vending machines that were not robbed although left unattended, and people stopping traffic to admire squirrels crossing the street. The land of milk and squirrels! I loved it!

After obtaining my BASc majoring in Electrical Engineering from the University of Toronto, I went to work at IBM Canada Ltd (*) in the software industry. I obtained an MBA with distinction by attending night school at York University.

I have managed uncounted numbers of people, and hired a number of brilliant men and women who have been tremendous contributors to the business and society. My biggest professional turn-on is the creation of high performance teams. I was able to do this several times, and I love my job for it. My team members told me they liked their job environment very much due to it, too.

Over the years I have been asked by many people to counsel them on the topics I have shared with you in this book, topics I reflected on over and over again, looking for wisdom and fine tuning. It's a lifetime work still in progress. I learned what I believe to be true through experimentation and experience, through sharing with friends and colleagues in other companies, through reflection on what I liked and didn't like in the way I was treated as an employee, discussions with people from many walks of life, and asking people who reported to me what worked for them. I don't see my approach as rocket science, but it's also not representative of what I have come across by way of management practice. I am hopeful that this book may help change society to something that I would feel more comfortable belonging to, and in the process allow employees to be treated more like they deserve.

I have taken all five Co-Active Coaching courses from CTI, and I am a certified Project Management Professional from PMI. I have received Outstanding Leadership Awards, Outstanding Technical Achievement Award, Patent Award, and consistently scored high morale employee surveys over the years. I am passionate about management and the development of the folks working with me, and the health of the teams I work in. I love being a leader, an agent of change.

I have a fabulous wife and a handful of children (five at the time of first publishing). I am a father by vocation so that means I am very busy with my kids, every day.

I am happy to tell you that I have a rich and satisfying life outside of work, and yes you can succeed both at work and home, if you are a manager. I am passionate about a long list of hobbies: I play chess, enjoy fly fishing (I tie my own flies), winemaking, photography, woodworking, and gardening.   My biggest challenge presently is learning Mandarin Chinese, that I would like to add to my Spanish, Italian, English and passable French. I like snorkeling, have an Open Water Diver certification. I like soccer, cycling and badminton. I like writing and inventing things.   I will improve at Go. Why such a long list of hobbies? Because life is short and meant to be lived passionately. Do these things really get done in spite of a full job and a full family life? Absolutely! It's about work life balance, applying the principles in this book so that I can squeeze the most out of my life. I hope this gets you thinking of how much time, really, there is in a day. How much fun you can have when you're living "high performance".

I sincerely hope my efforts have helped you in some way.   What you do is tremendously important.   Your impact on society is incalculable.   I wish you and your teams, success and fulfillment by all measures known and to be invented.

Most importantly, enjoy your job!

Fred Gandolfi

Markham, Canada
(you can reach me at fred.gandolfi@gmail.com)

 (*) The views expressed in this book are those of the author and not necessarily of IBM Canada Ltd.

Shortcuts to Greater Experience

There is no substitute for experience, and the lessons learned by the generous spilling of your own blood are the ones you truly won't forget, and may someday even master. But your teams, family, customer, manager and your health may suffer while you thrash about trying to figure out what to do with yourself and your teams, as I did. I offer you the following list of books and movies in the hope that the proper reflection on the lessons they offer may speed up the process for you – they taught me a lot.

Suggested Reading

"**Meditations**" by Marcus Aurelius will give you the humility you need, when your head gets too fat. There was a time this book was considered mandatory fare for the enlightened western gentleman.

"**Tuesdays with Morrie**" by Mitch Albom, reminds me of what matters in life. I believe that to be an effective manager and leader you need to be balanced, have perspective, and be in charge of your life. I read this book every six months.

For a complete resetting of perspectives, including convincing myself that my problems are trivial and solvable, I read "**Night**" by Elie Wiesel also every six months. It is a valuable reminder of man's potential to abuse power without limits or regard to the welfare of others, when moral values don't exist to curtail it. After you ground yourself in this book, and try to imagine a world where this can happen, all your problems and those of your people vanish into thin air. Then you give thanks for your life and with zeal and enthusiasms go enjoy all it has to offer you. Sometimes you need to look down and see true rock bottom below, to appreciate how close you are to the mountaintop.

I appreciate "**The World's Religions**", by Houston Smith. It shows you clearly and concisely, how every major religion is based on tolerance and respect. None allow for killing, and most are about the betterment of the self and the attainment of peace, purity of the soul. Clearly nobody following the spirit and intent of these religions could harm a fly. We have common ground on Religious intent, items where Dogma reigns over Logic and agreement is otherwise impossible? All religions tell you to be good and respectful of others? Wonderful! Then there is hope for cooperation, bonding, teaming and understanding everywhere in our lives, including the workplace. Read this book and learn what your fellow humans are up to, and don't be intimidated by those who appear to be different from you. They have more in common with you than you imagine.

Suggested Movies

"**The Fog of War: Eleven Lessons From the Life of Robert S. McNamara**" (2003) is a riveting account on Leadership under difficult circumstances, and a refreshing look at the perspectives facing an influential leader, and how he deals with them. I admire him very much. The lessons from this DVD, you ignore at your personal and professional peril.

"**Apollo 13**" (1995). This movie offers a wonderful portrayal by Tom Hanks, and Ed Harris of the difficulties of leadership.

"**The Straight Story**" (1999). This movie boosts your open mindedness about the intrinsic value of all people, and the resourcefulness of determined individuals. Your job as a manager and leader is to get them determined; they will manage the resourceful part.

"**Glengarry Glen Ross**" (1992). This is the movie you must watch to see professional manipulators in action. That way you can spot when it is being done to you, or to yours.

"**Office Space**" (1999). What may happen if you don't take this book to heart? ☺.

"**Butterfly Effect**" (2004). So many people are afraid of choosing the wrong thing, as if life had but a set of predictable, simple outcomes. I believe whatever comprises our experiences and persona today is a probabilistic miracle, and that is the way it was meant to be. I believe that all manner of insignificant events in our past or the past of others we came across (or didn't) have had a profound impact on our lives. We're not in control. We can't possibly know the evolving sets of choices any path will lay at our feet days or years from now. Do your best; let life happen and enjoy it.

I believe in the infinite possibilities that lie within ourselves, within the people who choose to let us lead them. You need focus, you need purpose. The rest is easy. I like these two quotes:

I am still puzzled as to how far the individual counts:
A lot, I fancy, if he pushes the right way.
                                    T .E. Lawrence (Lawrence of Arabia)
                                    May 15th, 1930

Our problems are man-made. Therefore they may be solved by man. And man can be as big as he wants. No problem of human destiny is beyond human beings.
                                    John F. Kennedy
                                    June 10th, 1963